Healthy and Natural Living in Chicago

Healthy and Natural Living in Chicago

The Best Alternative Resources in the City and Suburbs

Darlene E. Paris

CHICAGO REVIEW PRESS

Library of Congress Cataloging-in-Publication Data

Paris, Darlene E.
    Healthy and natural living in Chicago : the best alternative resources in the city and suburbs / Darlene E. Paris.
       p.   cm.
    Includes bibliographical references.
    ISBN 1-55652-295-9
      1. Alternative medicine—Illinois—Chicago Metropolitan Area—Directories.
I. Title.
R733.p35   1998
615.5'025'7731—dc21   98-7682
                                                                                    CIP

The author and the publisher of this book disclaim all liability incurred in connection with the use of the information contained in this book.

Prices and facilities are subject to change. We have made every effort to make this book as accurate as possible at the time of publication. Please call locations to get current information.

At the time of publication there were reports that the 847 area code, which covers the region north of Chicago to the Wisconsin border, might be split into two codes, 847 and 224. Please check all 847 numbers for accuracy.

© 1998 by Darlene E. Paris
All rights reserved

First edition
Published by Chicago Review Press, Incorporated
814 North Franklin Street
Chicago, Illinois 60610
ISBN 1-55652-295-9
Printed in the United States of America
5 4 3 2 1

Contents

Acknowledgments vii

Foreword, Bruno Cortis, M.D., F.A.C.C. ix

Introduction xiii

1. Holistic Health Care 1
2. Natural Pharmacies 33
3. Natural Food Shopping 43
4. Learning and Resource Centers 71
5. Meditation in Motion Classes 79
6. Relaxation Places 95
7. Earth-Friendly Stores 113
8. Organic and Vegetarian Restaurants 125
9. Groups and Publications 137

Appendix A: Abbreviations of Professional Credentials 145

Appendix B: Chain Store Locations in Chicago and the Suburbs 147

Glossary 167

To existence

Acknowledgments

There were several people who served as midwives as I labored with the creation of this book. I would like to thank Gary Walls, Ph.D., who helped me rediscover parts of myself that I had forgotten. I would also like to thank Sue Telingator for recommending that I write this book, and Cynthia Sherry, my editor, for her belief in my ability to pull a book of this magnitude together. Also, I'd like to thank Lisa Rosenthal, my project editor, for her meticulous attention to detail that helped in organizing the various resources that are included in this book.

Many thanks go to my mother, who may not have understood my determination to complete this project, but offered her loving support anyway, and to my sister, Deidre, for her prayers and tacit admiration. Thanks to Niketan, who opened his heart and home so that I could write various chapters in a space of meditation and who gave me the gift of a laptop computer on which I completed the final chapters. Thanks to the many holistic health professionals I met during my research: Bruno Cortis, M.D., Pauline Harding, M.D., Ed Kaleolani Spencer, R.N., Taf Paulson, D.D.S., and Ray Bayley, D.C., D.A.C.B.N., who contributed names of professionals in the area who believe in holistic health and who have, themselves, assisted hundreds of patients on their journey to wellness. Thanks also to the various people who took time to give me information on the resources that are included in this guide.

Special thanks go to the staff members of *Conscious Choice: The Journal of Ecology & Natural Living*, Aliess Brady, Sondra Brigandi, Leslie Limburg, and publisher Jim Slama, for their support and contributions to this book. Also a big thank-you to Sharon Steffenson, editor at *YogaChicago*. Thank you, Dharma, for reminding me that existence takes care. And last, but not least, thank you, Jessica, for your friendship, love, and constant support.

Foreword

We are assisting in a profound transformation in medicine: from the old doctor-centered medicine we are now moving toward a new era of patient-centered medicine. In the old model, the patient was supposed to obey the physician's orders blindly, but, in the new model, the patient enters into a partnership with the physician for a common goal—the maintenance of health and the prolongation of an active, joyful life.

The most important aspect of medicine is not the medication itself but the patient/physician relationship. Such a relationship is often cold and professional, probably because the physician does not know the patient as a person and vice versa.

If the patient thinks that the physician knows everything and the physician believes that he or she knows everything, where is there any room for what the patient knows? Aren't we doctors also human? Don't we too have a heart?

Let's talk to each other. We have something to do. We must do it together. So I wrote in my journal: "The reason we don't understand and love each other is because I talk to you like a doctor, but professional language won't break any barriers. There is in me a sensible heart, like you have. I want you to know it. Until you find out what I am like—human and vulnerable—we will not understand each other. We physicians don't just deal with disease; we deal with people who have disease."

The patient/physician relationship involves much more than a mere description of symptoms. A patient's symptoms come from living life; therefore, treating the symptoms must include touching the patient's life on other levels—mental, emotional, and spiritual.

Only when all the barriers separating the patient and doctor have fallen can the real work of healing begin. This is a collaborative effort as necessary to the physician as to the patient.

Health is not simply the absence of disease. In terms of the total human being, health implies our physical, mental, and spiritual dimensions. Most of today's medicine treats only the physical.

How can there be health without spirituality? Can the body live without the soul that makes it? The spiritual powers within far surpass any others. Transcendent, they lift all of humanity up and honor the spirit of God within us.

The physician, with a spiritual orientation, helps the patient understand that disease can be a wanted experience, can help the patient discover why it happened so that the healing process can begin, explains the intimate connection between mind and body, and helps evoke the patient's own healing powers.

When the patient becomes responsible for his or her own health and works with the physician as a partner, we have a solid foundation for holistic medicine.

The medicine of the future will be more human, spiritual, and love-oriented: the real medicine is the medicine of the whole person.

When I began the practice of holistic medicine, I was in search of teachers, of colleagues with whom to relate; I imagine that patients went through the same struggle in search of holistic physicians.

Now the book of Darlene E. Paris fills that gap, offering a guide to the best alternative healing resources in the city and suburbs. This book provides all the information necessary for you to find the right doctor, a person with whom you can relate and can trust, who will listen and give you the time to express your feelings, clarify your doubts, help you to go through illness—a doctor who provides hope, evoking your spirituality as a path to recovery; a doctor who is a teacher, a friend, and who is not afraid to express care and love.

In *Healthy and Natural Living in Chicago*, you will find the natural pharmacies that will help you maintain your health with vitamins and minerals. In addition, the book offers a guide to natural food shopping and to learning resource centers where you can take classes that will assist you with your personal growth and spiritual healing. Paris also includes other resources like yoga centers, massage spas, and vegetarian restaurants.

This book is informative, enriching, and inspirational. It will help you design a path to higher levels of health and to a happy, joyful life.

Bruno Cortis, M.D., F.A.C.C.
Author of *Heart & Soul: A Psychological and Spiritual Guide to Preventing and Healing Heart Disease*

Introduction

When I told a friend who lives on a farm in Michigan that I was writing a book entitled *Healthy and Natural Living in Chicago*, he was amazed. "That's impossible," he replied. "I've lived in that city for twenty years and the allergies I developed proves that there's just no way that you can live in Chicago with good health. That's why I packed my gear and moved to the country," he explained.

I could understand his point. In fact, the *Rating Guide to Environmentally Healthy Metro Areas* by Robert Weinhold listed two towns where I've spent the majority of my life as being extremely hazardous to my health—Gary, Indiana, and Chicago. I have to admit that Chicago is not the healthiest environment. Heck, not only is the environment less than ideal, but just living in the area can be amazingly stressful. Morning and evening rush hours are a harrowing experience. And once you get to work, the scenario can be just as bad— fewer people and an ever-growing amount of work. And as the workload increases, so does the stress. Doctors tell us that stress is one of the major causes of illness.

Despite its many faults, I love living in the Chicago area, and if you love living here as much as I do, you'll want to find ways to keep healthy so you can continue to enjoy whatever you love most. The good news is that despite all the pollution and stress, there are numerous health-related resources in the Chicago metropolitan area to help you live healthier. The resources I'm referring to emphasize holistic well-being; that is, taking care of your mind, body, and spirit.

One of the ways some physicians and other health-care professionals are helping people stay healthy is by incorporating alternative medicine, which includes therapies like massage, acupuncture, naturopathy, and yoga, into a Western medical regime. More and more health-care professionals are realizing that the human body can heal itself. A 1993 study presented in the *New England Journal of Medicine* by David Eisenberg, M.D., concluded that one in three Americans use some form of unconventional therapy.

Alternative medical practices are now being used by some physicians working at Chicago area hospitals such as Northwestern Memorial Hospital, Rush-Presbyterian, St. Luke's Medical Center, Illinois Masonic Medical Center, and Mercy Medical Center. The health professionals at these hospitals use a mixture of healing therapies to treat patients and integrate alternative treatments with conventional medicine. They call this method of healing patients integrative medicine. No matter what it's called, more health professionals are realizing that the body has the ability to heal itself and that there are practical ways that a doctor, working with a patient, can achieve wellness.

Since health care is rapidly changing, one of the things that most patients are discovering is that they need to take an active role in maintaining their own health. If you are someone who is interested in taking more responsibility for the health of your mind, body, and spirit, then this book is for you.

The resources in this book have been culled over a period of seven years. Some of them derive from health resources that have helped me achieve good health and peace of mind.

Other sources of information come from my two years of experience as editor of a now-defunct holistic health newsletter entitled *Her Spirit Rises*. I've also collected information from people who are in the field of alternative medicine, such as Ed Spencer, R.N., a holistic health-care provider who has practiced in the field of alternative medicine for many years, and other professionals who are proponents of mind-body medicine like Pauline Harding, M.D., Ray Bayley, D.C., D.A.C.B.N., and Taf Paulson, D.D.S. These individuals have graciously shared their lists of referral contacts so that I could include them in this book. I have also collected the names of resources from staff members at such publications as *Conscious Choice: The Journal of Ecology & Natural Living*, *YogaChicago*, and other publications with the theme of alternative health and natural living.

While the people and businesses listed in this resource guide are based on referrals and/or personally selected, listings do not constitute endorsements, and I encourage you to do your own investigations. The road to wellness is a personal, private affair, and it's important that you select the resources that are best for you. *Healthy and Natural Living in Chicago* is designed to point you in the right direction.

Appendix A gives a list of all credential abbreviations used in this book. Keep in mind that some of these healing arts do not have state certification programs. For example, the state of Illinois does not regulate massage therapists by licensure. The city of Chicago requires its massage therapists to obtain licenses, but massage therapists who work in the suburbs are regulated by the local ordinances of the cities, villages, or counties in which they practice. Before selecting a practitioner, call to get an explanation of his or her qualifications.

Appendix B lists the locations of major chain stores in Chicago and the suburbs such as General Nutrition Centers and The Body Shop.

Within each chapter, you'll find the listings organized alphabetically within each of four geographical regions:

Chicago
North/Northwest Suburbs
South/Southwest Suburbs
Western Suburbs

Each business listing consists of an address and telephone number and, when possible, the hours of operation, as well as a description of the services offered and prices for some services. However, it's best to call ahead to verify that this information is still current. A glossary in the back of the book will help those who are less familiar with the alternative healthcare terminology used in this book.

Although this book represents several of the holistic health resources in the area, it does not include all of them. The field of alternative health care is forever changing, and I'm sure that I have missed several people and places that are dedicated to helping people live a more healthy and happy life.

Remember, the condition of your health shouldn't be left in the hands of your doctor alone. There are things that you can do to increase your sense of well-being. Whether you're feeling on top of the world or battling a chronic disease such as cancer, you should be aware of the different resources in the area that will help uplift your mind, body, and spirit. Good luck on your journey to good health. Your time on earth is precious. Be well.

Darlene E. Paris
September 1998

1 Holistic Health Care

Have you ever been to a medical doctor and wondered if he knew you were sitting in the room? This is the feeling I experienced almost every time I visited my former doctor, who was steeped in the traditional way of practicing medicine. Even though he and I would exchange small talk before he inquired about my condition, he never really seemed to notice me. Once I explained my health challenges, he would immediately listen to my heart, look into my ears, and then ask me to open my mouth and say, "Ahhhh." After examining my body for five minutes, he would miraculously determine the nature of my condition, usually a virus, and then prescribe medication. End of visit. He never bothered to ask me anything like "How's your stress level?" or "How's that new job going?" or "What's happening with your diet?" The answers to these questions may have given him tremendous insight into my sudden decline in health. It seemed that all my doctor really cared about was prescribing drugs to ease my pain so that he could quickly escort me out of his office.

This kind of treatment from my doctor was the catalyst for my quest to find another one. I was no longer interested in taking prescriptions to temporarily relieve illness or mask pain. I was in search of a doctor who saw my virus as a symptom of something gone awry in my body, and who would help me understand the real cause or causes behind my ill health.

Then about six years ago, a minister friend of mine named Reverend Marsha—a staunch advocate of acupuncture, colonics, and herbal remedies—told me about a group of health-care providers who believed in holistic health. I had never heard the term *holistic* before, but whatever it was, it sounded a lot better than the word *conventional*. She later explained that these health-care providers, who realized that patients were comprised of mind, body, and spirit and that a balance of all three was necessary to maintain good health, focused on treating the whole person, not just the disease.

I later learned that health-care providers who embraced this mind-body-spirit approach to wellness were not only medical doctors, but also lay people who practiced a wide variety of healing arts.

In this chapter, you'll find some of the discoveries I made during my six-year search for alternative health-care providers. You will read about holistic clinics in the area and the expertise of their staff. You'll also find medical doctors, doctors of osteopathic medicine, chiropractors, dentists, acupuncturists, massage therapists, psychiatrists and psychologists, counselors, and other practitioners who believe in holistic health. I've included a list of holistic clinics located in the city and suburbs. Holistic clinics have a range of licensed health-care providers on staff. Some even employ medical doctors who serve as medical directors. These physicians are there to help you choose the best combination of holistic health-care treatment for your particular health challenges. You'll notice that I have not listed office hours for any of the holistic clinics. Most of these places operate on a flexible time schedule because some of the practitioners work at other health-care facilities.

This chapter also lists some of the best holistic health-care providers in the Chicago area. All the practitioners included in the book are either licensed or trained professionals and were recommended by sources who have either used holistic health care for several years or are longtime participants in the industry themselves and have recommended other practitioners with comparable talent. Many of these practitioners work out of their homes and/or make house calls; therefore, office hours are not provided throughout nor are addresses.

Although I have taken time to personally talk to most of the people listed in this book, I advise that you call the professional yourself for a mini-interview. The purpose of the call is to find out more about the physician or practitioner's method of practice and to arrange an appointment to meet him or her in person.

When you visit a professional for your first appointment, don't expect to be in the office at 9:00 A.M. and out thirty minutes later. This health expert is serious and committed to your well-being, so he or she will need extra time to understand you and your health issues a little better. So be warned and ask the health-care provider you choose the amount of time needed for your first and subsequent appointments.

Holistic Health Centers

Chicago

AIDS Alternative Health Project
4753 N. Broadway, Suite 1118
Chicago, IL 60640
(773) 561-2800
Founded in 1986, this not-for-profit organization began with a group of massage therapists and acupuncturists who were concerned that HIV patients were not receiving compassionate hands-on care from the medical community. To fill this need, they started performing body work on these patients in a basement. Today, twenty-two different kinds of healing therapies are offered by volunteer practitioners and physicians in a holistic center located within the Uptown Bank Building on the city's North Side. Some of the therapies include Chinese medicine, nutritional counseling, massage therapy, chiropractic treatment, and acupuncture. Physicians are available to assist patients with choosing the appropriate therapies. A sliding fee scale is available for patients who qualify.

A new addition to this practice is the for-profit Alternative Health Partners. Open to the public, this practice combines Western and Eastern medicine. Contact them at 4753 N. Broadway, Suite 1126, Chicago, IL 60640, (773) 561-2800.

Alternative Health Partners
4753 N. Broadway, Suite 1126
Chicago, IL 60640
(773) 561-3400
A division of Ravenswood Hospital Medical Center, the staff at this clinic consists of a medical doctor, chiropractors, massage therapists, a holistic counselor, and acupuncturists. Specializing in women's health issues, practitioners at this clinic use complementary therapies such as massage therapy,

herbal therapy, and acupuncture to treat such conditions as menopause, premenstrual syndrome, and emotional and psychological issues that accompany menopause and pregnancy. They also treat musculoskeletal and respiratory conditions and offer nutritional therapy.

The Alternative Medicine Clinic
8 S. Michigan Avenue, Suite 1418
Chicago, IL 60603
(312) 456-3000
The staff at this South Loop clinic includes a traditional doctor, chiropractor, and an acupuncturist who combine their skills to help patients achieve good health. Douglass Finlayson, M.D., has been practicing medicine for over thirty years and uses allopathic remedies as well as nutritional therapies to treat his patients. Nicholas Leroy, D.C., a chiropractic physician and acupuncturist, takes a holistic approach to women's health issues, and Frank Yurasek, M.A., Ac.P., an acupuncturist with training in herbology and homeopathy, also treats patients using Oriental massage. Other therapies offered at this clinic include the Alexander technique, chelation therapy, colon therapy, constructive living coaching, craniosacral therapy, flower essence therapy, medical qi gong, physiotherapy, and tai chi instruction.

American WholeHealth
990 W. Fullerton Avenue, Suite 300
Chicago, IL 60614
(773) 296-6700

American WholeHealth/North Loop Chiropractic
150 E. Huron, Suite 1100
Chicago, IL 60611
(312) 951-1117
The largest holistic health-care facility in the Chicago metropolitan area, the professionals at this center practice integrative medicine—a melding of conventional and alternative

therapies to help patients achieve good health. Staff members include medical doctors and chiropractors who work with licensed herbologists, massage therapists, and a host of other holistic practitioners, including an acupuncturist, nutritional counselor, and naprapath. These professionals take part in the patient's Healing Path—a tailor-made wellness program designed by the patient and physician that involves education, specialized testing, medical treatment, and lifestyle changes. They also have an excellent education department that includes an outreach program where healing professionals from the center lecture at various places throughout the Chicago area.

Biosystems Wellness Center
401 W. Ontario, Suite 200
Chicago, IL 60610
(312) 642-4674
Because the staff at this medically supervised clinic believe that the future of health care hinges on preventive medicine, physical fitness is the cornerstone of their clinic. Tom Klein, M.D., an expert on AIDS care, works with a husband-and-wife team of personal trainers to assist patients in taking preventive measures to remain healthy. In addition to providing one-on-one fitness training, they also offer other services such as nutritional counseling, hormone testing, massage therapy, and Shiatsu. Their forty-eight-day cellular detoxification program is extremely effective and involves the use of homeopathic remedies to internally cleanse the body.

Chicago Center for Chronic Disorders
636 S. Michigan Avenue
Chicago, IL 60605
(312) 431-1475
This wellness center is a wonderful healing place for individuals with such conditions as heart disease, asthma, diabetes, hypertension, and arthritis. The members of this staff are com-

mitted to eradicating these disorders not by administering drugs or surgery, but by helping to enliven the inner intelligence of the body so that healing occurs naturally from within. Treatment at this center, which is located in the old Blackstone Hotel, includes a three-week residency program where patients learn the effects of consciousness on physiology and the fundamentals of nutrition plus how to adjust their diets. Patients also get information on herbal supplementation usage and an understanding of the relationship between the health of an individual and the health of society.

Integrative Therapies
2334 W. Lawrence Avenue, Suite 216
Chicago, IL 60625
(773) 275-9940
An alternative health clinic since 1982, this place integrates body therapy, Chinese medicine, massage, and energetic therapy. Services offered include Rolfing, structural therapy, acupuncture, herbology, Hawaiian energetics, craniosacral therapy, and Gestalt therapy.

Karyn's Inner Beauty Center
3304 N. Lincoln Avenue
Chicago, IL 60657
(773) 281-7708
Karyn Calabrese, the owner of this holistic health-care facility and a well-known advocate in the Chicago area for holistic health and living, says that her inner healing center offers all the services she uses to keep her own body looking young and feeling healthy. The center, located just across the street from Calabrese's vegan restaurant, Karyn's Fresh Corner, offers colon therapy; oxygen bathing, a technique that cleanses and detoxifies the body on a cellular level; and massage treatments. Calabrese holds classes in yoga, tai chi, chi kung, ballet, and meditation. She also teaches workshops throughout the year entitled Nature's Weight Loss System and Nature's Healing

System. The center is open seven days a week from 9:00 A.M. to 9:00 P.M.

Lincoln Square Health Clinic
2334 W. Lawrence, Suite 209
Chicago, IL 60625
(773) 769-6400

The place to go for compassionate health care, the owners of this ten-year-old business are a wife-and-husband team who offer an array of holistic therapies to improve health. Terry Kay, D.C., a chiropractor, naprapath, and colon therapist, uses her knowledge of the healing arts plus nutritional counseling to treat patients. Her husband, Bob Kearney, is a body worker and offers craniosacral therapy, muscle work, and orthopedic massage, plus structural and trigger-point therapies. In addition to working with each other, these holistic health providers also work with a network of holistic practitioners in the area, including a homeopath who gives homeopathic counseling.

Strong Spirit Wellness Center
938 W. Nelson, Third Floor
Chicago, IL 60657
(773) 296-8410

One of the best holistic health-care programs in the city, Strong Spirit is a division of Illinois Masonic Hospital and offers a comprehensive program of complementary healing therapies. Physicians, nurses, and alternative therapists work cooperatively to improve the patient's health and well-being. But the real goal of this health-care facility is to empower patients to take charge of their mental, emotional, and spiritual health. Education programs consist of weekly classes in tai chi and yoga. They also offer workshops on a quarterly basis such as Reiki and women's drumming. The healing arts program, held every Tuesday, allows patients to experience various healing modalities, including Hawaiian energetics and craniosacral therapy. There's also a special healing arts program for HIV and oncology patients that includes a support group.

Ton Shen Health
2131 S. Archer, Suites B and C
Chicago, IL 60616
(312) 842-2775
Sixth-generation master traditional Chinese herbalist Zhengang Guo is the director of this clinic, which specializes in traditional Chinese medicine. Guo works with a team of board-certified acupuncturists and a practitioner who specializes in Tuina massage, a Chinese system of massage that involves the stimulation of the body's acupressure points and meridians. An herbal pharmacy, stocked with family and classic formulas, is on the premises and only services those customers with prescriptions. Guo also offers advanced herbal training at the clinic for Chinese medicine practitioners and other health professionals.

Waveland Wellness Center
1346 W. Waveland Avenue
Chicago, IL 60613
(773) 935-5050
This place has medical doctors on staff who work with a wide array of alternative therapists. Physicians specialize in nutritional medicine, disease prevention, stress management, and anti-aging. They also offer a smoking cessation program and nutritional therapy for cancer patients. Some other forms of therapy include: Chinese medicine, acupuncture, herbology, Feldenkrais, massage therapy, colon therapy, chiropractic treatment, nutritional counseling, psychotherapy, yoga, meditation, orthobionomy, biofeedback, stress management, and holistic psychiatry.

Wellness Associates of Chicago
706 W. Junior Terrace
Chicago, IL 60613
(773) 935-6377
Martha Howard, M.D., the medical director at this place, is board certified in family practice and also uses traditional Chinese medicine to treat patients. She works with other professionals who provide light-assisted biofeedback, general herbal medicine, internal massage, and naprapathy.

Wellspace
Mercy Hospital and Medical Center
2525 S. Michigan Avenue
Chicago, IL 60616
(312) 567-2259
The licensed professionals at this facility—one of the first centers of its kind in the Chicago area located within a hospital—help patients alleviate stress. Practitioners use various treatments of body work including the Feldenkrais method and zero balancing. They also teach meditation. A five-week program called Lesstress teaches patients various techniques for eliminating stress.

White Crane Wellness Center
1355 W. Foster Avenue
Chicago, IL 60657
(773) 271-9001
For those aged fifty and older, the White Crane Wellness Center is an independent not-for-profit organization founded by seniors to provide services to older adults interested in improving their health. White Crane—an Asian symbol for long life and good health—offers a number of holistic services such as tai chi and yoga classes. Volunteer practitioners provide acupuncture and chiropractic and massage treatments in addition to blood pressure, cancer, and podiatric screenings. They also offer weekly nutrition classes and other health-oriented pro-

grams. The annual fee for a White Crane membership is $10 and includes a monthly newsletter and activity calendar, invitations to special events, reduced rates at a number of local restaurants and shops, discounts at select Northside Osco pharmacies, plus a $3 admission fee for classes. A Gold Card membership fee is $100 and includes all the benefits of an annual membership, plus free admission to all classes and workshops and discounts on massage therapy sessions.

North/Northwest Suburbs

Center for the Healing Arts
650 Vernon Avenue
Glencoe, IL 60022
(847) 835-6207
Under the direction of Toni Bark, M.D., a licensed physician trained in classical homeopathy, this place offers massage, psychotherapy, art and play therapy for children with special needs, pediatric occupational therapy, Feldenkrais treatments, chiropractic services, podiatric services, and acupuncture services.

Center for Holistic Medicine
240 Saunders Road
Riverwoods, IL 60015
(847) 236-1701
The practitioners at this center, the oldest holistic health-care clinic in the Chicago area, practice integrative health care using Ayurveda, Chinese medicine, homeopathy, nutritional counseling, psychology, acupuncture, Shiatsu, meditation, tai chi, and yoga. They also specialize in the holistic treatment of acute and chronic ailments such as respiratory and sinus problems, gastrointestinal disorders, candidiasis, hypertension, and arthritis. The center has an education department that offers courses in vegetarian cooking, Hatha yoga, and stress-reduc-

tion techniques. They also have a community outreach program where practitioners lecture at various places in and surrounding Chicago.

The Himalayan Institute's Holistic Health Center
1505 Greenwood Road
Glenview, IL 60025
(847) 486-0400
The Institute has a holistic physician on staff, Dale Buegel, M.D., who specializes in homeopathic medicine and assists patients in choosing alternative therapies to enhance their health. Patients also work with a host of on-staff licensed holistic practitioners including a massage therapist, a Chinese medicine practitioner, and a holistic psychotherapist. The types of services offered include Ayurveda counseling, acupuncture, neuro-muscular and myofascial treatments, craniosacral therapy, neurolinguistic programming, hypnosis, dreamwork, meditation, and Bach flower essence therapy. This place also offers herbal and aromatherapy body wraps.

Kusala Healing Center
484 Central Avenue, Suite 301
Highland Park, IL 60035
(847) 433-4410
Energy field work is one of the preferred treatment methods at this holistic center located in downtown Highland Park. Professionals use healing touch, energy balancing, Reiki, and acupressure. Flower essence therapy is also available. Practitioners also offer classes and workshops on a monthly basis where they introduce and explain various holistic healing modalities.

The Miro Center for Integrative Medicine
1639 Orrington Avenue
Evanston, IL 60201
(847) 733-9900
Formerly the Evanston Holistic Center, this newly structured

alternative health clinic is the only place of its kind that makes holistic health care affordable by offering financial assistance to patients who qualify. Directed by Connie Catellani, M.D., a physician on staff at Rush North Shore Hospital in Skokie, the professionals at this not-for-profit clinic take a holistic approach to Western medicine, osteopathy, homeopathy, herbology, Chinese medicine, manipulation therapies, nutritional counseling, psychology, pranic healing, aromatherapy, Reiki, and yoga. There are also annual memberships available that include discounts on classes, seminars, and purchases at the apothecary. Miro's education department features an ongoing series of classes and lectures on holistic health plus free weekly meditation sessions.

Northwest Wellness Center
909 E. Palatine Road
Palatine, IL 60067
(847) 776-1400
Licensed professionals at this one-stop clinic for health and well-being offer alternative health treatments as well as classes on holistic health. Treatments include acupuncture, acupressure, skeletal manipulation, therapeutic massage, psychotherapy, and nutritional counseling. They also offer classes in tai chi and qi gong.

Randolph-Shambaugh Clinic
Environmental Health Center
2500 W. Higgins Road, Suite 1170
Hoffman Estates, IL 60195
(847) 519-7772
Physicians at this health-care facility treat patients who are environmentally sensitive. Trained professionals conduct tests for food, inhalant, and chemical sensitivities as well as give hormonal evaluations, provide treatment for candidiasis, and offer nutritional analysis and counseling.

The Wellness Group
707 Lake Cook Road, Suite 320
Deerfield, IL 60015
(847) 559-9355
A small but intimate center where patients get good holistic health care, this center offers chiropractic treatments, colon therapy, aromatherapy, massage therapy, and neurolinguistic programming sessions. Patients also come for spa services such as waxing, body wraps, and facials.

South/Southwest Suburbs

Health Choices
18155 Roy Street
Lansing, IL 60438
(708) 474-9298
A natural health service center that offers private blood testing, this facility also offers acupuncture, aromatherapy, ear candling, massage treatments, Reiki sessions, plus herbal and aromatherapy wraps. There's also a retail area inside the center that features an array of music, books, jewelry, crystals, candles, incense, and a small collection of books and CDs. Audio and video tapes are also available for rent.

Insight Awareness Center
18112 Martin Avenue
Homewood, IL 60430
(708) 957-1284
Located in the heart of downtown Homewood, this place offers a full range of retail, educational, and healing services. Staffed by two full-time certified massage therapists, this holistic center provides aromatherapy treatments, on-site chair massage, foot reflexology, lymphatic massage, infant massage instruction, and full body massage. John Sparks, a Reiki mas-

ter and massage therapist, combines the healing power of energy field work with body work. He also instructs Reiki classes. The center hosts a variety of special classes and workshops each year including Angel Tea, A Course in Miracles, Drumming Circle, Guided Meditation, and a Reiki support group. A quarterly newsletter keeps clients abreast of the center's latest offerings.

The Wellness Center
23162 West Lincoln Highway
Plainfield, IL 60544
(815) 439-1208
The most intriguing aspect of this center is that it's located in a log cabin. Its rustic veneer, reminiscent of a simpler, less stressful way of life, and the expertise of its staff make it an ideal place for healing. The owner, Anita Schiavi, is a certified massage therapist who is also trained in reflexology, Thai massage, zero balancing, craniosacral therapy, neuro-muscular therapy, therapeutic touch, and specialized kinesiology (a technique used to relieve visual inhibition). There are ten other therapists on staff who offer various types of body work including manual lymphatic drainage. Classes in tai chi, chi kung, and Iyengar yoga, a style of Hatha yoga that involves the use of props, are also taught on a regular basis.

Western Suburbs

Caring Medical and Rehabilitation Services
715 Lake Street, Suite 600
Oak Park, IL 60301
(708) 848-7789
This clinic's physician, Ross Hauser, M.D., combines his knowledge of conventional medicine with more natural therapies to treat illnesses. This is one of the few places in the Chicago area that offers ozone therapy for treating such conditions as herpes, hepatitis, HIV, and candidiasis. Other treatments include photoluminescence (ultraviolet blood irradiation), which detoxifies the body and treats viral illnesses; prolotherapy for chronic pain; metabolic typing; chelation treatments; and anti-aging regimens. This clinic is among a handful of centers in the country conducting research in the use of intradermal bee venom injections for treating multiple sclerosis. Nutritional counseling is also available by a licensed clinical nutritionist.

Center for Integrative Treatment and Biochemical Nutrition
715 Lake Street, Suite 106
Oak Park, IL 60301
(708) 383-3800
This is the place to go for treatment of such ailments as chronic fatigue syndrome, depression, insomnia, joint pain, and ADD (Attention Deficit Disorder). Paul Dunn, M.D., and his wife, Katherine, a licensed clinical nutritionist, have been treating chronic conditions naturally for more than thirty years. The doctor treats patients by using conventional treatments as well as homeopathic remedies, nutritional supplements, and nutritional counseling. A proponent of preventive medicine, Dr. Dunn also recommends relaxation techniques as well as exercise to improve and maintain good health.

Naperville Holistic Health Clinic
1280 Iroquois Drive, Suite 200
Naperville, IL 60563
(630) 369-1220
This clinic is recommended for patients who have had little success with conventional medicine. It's also a favorite healing place for heart patients and individuals who have been diagnosed with cancer. Some of the holistic treatments offered include environmental medicine, hormone rebalancing, live blood video-microscopy, chelation therapy, oxidative therapies, Bach flower remedies, nutritional therapy, and homeopathy. They also specialize in natural ways to treat Attention Deficit Disorder and depression. Medical director Robert C. Filice, M.D., also offers seminars to patients on various subjects pertaining to holistic health.

Ton Shen Health
665 Pasquinelli Drive, Suite 203
Westmont, IL 60559
(630) 789-2350
See the Ton Shen Health listing under Chicago for complete information.

The Whole Life Center
40 E. 31st Street
La Grange Park, IL 60526
(708) 352-7212
The health professionals at this holistic health-care facility use a blend of Western and Chinese medicine to treat patients. The medical director of the center, Lorene Wu, M.D., is board certified in family practice, but also uses acupuncture, acupressure, and herbology to treat patients. She works with Qiying Jiang, O.M.D. (Oriental Medical Doctor), who specializes in gynecology and pediatrics. Other services offered at the clinic include massage therapy, Reiki, nutritional counseling, and detoxification programs.

Holistic Practitioners

Acupuncture

Darryl Brayboy
Winnetka
(847) 441-6157

Pam Mills
Chicago
(773) 868-4064

Althea Northage-Orr
Chicago
(773) 975-1655

Dan Plovanich
Chicago
(773) 871-0342

Mei Ling Qian
Chicago
(312) 791-0025

Mary J. Rogel
Chicago
(773) 955-9643

Patti Trimble
Chicago
(773) 275-9949

Body Work

Robert Ahrens
Evanston
(847) 328-7174
Rolfing.

Lisa Alamar
Oak Park
(708) 383-5094
Structural therapy for athletes.

Leigh Ankrum
Chicago
(773) 880-1456
Craniosacral therapy, neuro-muscular massage, and structural therapy.

Jay Arovas
Chicago
(773) 472-1373
Massage therapy and Reiki.

Berlina R. Baker
Chicago
(773) 994-6323
Reflexology.

Darryl Brayboy
Winnetka
(847) 441-6157
Shiatsu.

Courtney Brown
Chicago
(773) 878-3865
Alexander technique.

Danita Brown
Homewood
(708) 481-9085
Massage therapy.

John Chamness
Morton Grove
(847) 965-5695
Massage therapy.

Larry Clemmons
Chicago
(312) 368-0104
Reflexology.

Nancy Curulewski
Carol Stream/Frankfort
(815) 469-3960
Craniosacral therapy, infant massage instruction, massage therapy, and reflexology.

Allan Davidson
Chicago
(773) 486-6857
Rolfing.

Barbara Drummond
Oakbrook/Waukegan
(847) 336-3066
Rolfing.

Sharon Fullington
Libertyville
(847) 680-9013
Thai massage and Shiatsu for pregnant women and clients who are in drug or alcohol recovery.

Karen Giles
Downers Grove
(630) 434-9960
Rolfing.

Carla Gorsky
Green Oaks/Libertyville
(847) 367-8842
Massage therapy, specializing in the treatment of chronic pain.

Deirdre Hill
Chicago
(773) 488-5877
Oriental massage.

Susan McConnell
Chicago
(773) 271-0689
Hakomi.

Liz McCormick
Oak Park
(708) 383-7438
Aromatherapy massage and Thai massage.

Suzanne Mitchem, R.N.
Tinley Park
(708) 429-9666
Massage therapy.

Brian Moore
Chicago
(800) 282-1222
Rolfing.

Althea Northage-Orr
Chicago
(773) 975-1655
Structural therapy.

Linda Paschall
Des Plaines
(847) 803-6576
Massage therapy.

Donald Soule
Chicago
(312) 645-1880
Rolfing.

Ed Kaleolani Spencer, R.N.
Chicago
(773) 275-9940
Craniosacral therapy, structural therapy, and rolfing.

Ariana Mariah and
Geoffrey Stahlka
Evanston
(847) 492-9624
Massage therapy, Krashada acupressure, and craniosacral therapy.

Robert Sturm
Chicago
(773) 764-9864
Lomi Lomi, massage therapy, tantric Shiatsu, watsu, and Zen Shiatsu.

Suhail J. U-Deen
Chicago
(773) 548-1365
Manipulation therapies.

Holly Whedbee
Chicago
(773) 275-9940
Structural therapy and massage therapy.

Soham Annette Wilkerson
Chicago
(773) 381-9606
Craniosacral therapy, infant massage instruction, and massage therapy.

Chinese Medicine Practitioners

Claudette Baker
527 Forest Avenue
Evanston, IL 60202
(847) 866-8116

Joseph Lee
702 W. 31st Street
Chicago, IL 60616
(312) 791-9898
655 Pasquinelli Drive
Unit 201
Westmont, IL 60559
(630) 325-9888

Mary Helen Lee
White Moon Healing Center
1309 W. Albion Avenue
Chicago, IL 60626
(773) 743-5229

Althea Northage-Orr
Chicago Center for Psychophysical Healing
1522 W. Nelson Avenue
Chicago, IL 60657
(773) 975-1655

Chih-Wei Rei, D.C.
3060 Ogden Avenue
Suite 110
Lisle, IL 60532
(630) 357-7320

Chiropractors

Ray Bayley, D.C., D.A.C.B.N.
Healing Hands
4242 N. Sheridan Road
Suite 117
Chicago, IL 60613
(773) 281-7100

Susan Borrelli, D.C., and Ann Generillia, D.C.
Chiropractic for Life
1961 Farragut Avenue
Chicago, IL 60640
(773) 878-8933
Network spinal analysis.

Sue Brown, D.C.
Essence Quality of Life Center
25 W. 330 Geneva Road
Carol Stream, IL 60188
(630) 690-6080
Network spinal analysis.

Susan DeFrain, D.C.
Peotone Chiropractic Natural Health Center, Ltd.
107 W. Main Street
Peotone, IL 60468
(708) 258-9600

Dale Dunn, D.C.
P.O. Box 1130
Oak Park, IL 60304
(708) 386-8822

Daniel Fedeli, D.C.
The Balancing Center
1871 N. Clybourn Avenue
Chicago, IL 60614
(773) 327-3333
Upper cervical techniques.

Mats R. Gunnars, D.C.
2320 W. Peterson, Suite 405
Chicago, IL 60659
(773) 262-2424

Asar Ha-Pi, D.N., D.C.
New Horizon Health Services
1737 S. Michigan Avenue
Suite 100

Chicago, IL 60616
(312) 939-7246

Christine Hoch, D.C.
Natural Health Chiropractic Center
9031 W. 151st Street
Orland Park, IL 60462
(708) 403-9450

Steven Holcomb, D.C.
Natural Medicine Clinic
213 Hywood Lane
Bolingbrook, IL 60440
(630) 378-0610

Clifford L. Kearns, D.C., D.N.B.H.E.
2223 W. Schaumburg Road
Schaumburg, IL 60194
(847) 301-8585

Isabel Munoz, D.N., D.C.
Evanston
(847) 256-7105
Specializing in treating kyphosis and scoliosis; also offers cancer therapy using acupuncture.

Andrew Pasminski, D.N., D.C.
Family Health Resources
1342 W. Belmont Avenue
Chicago, IL 60657
(773) 477-2225

Lori Portnoy, D.C.
954 W. Armitage Avenue
Chicago, IL 60614
(773) 248-2323

Liselotte Schuster, D.C.
Schuster Chiropractic
1535 Lake Cook Road
Suite 312
Northbrook, IL 60062
(847) 509-9067

Jack Taylor, D.C.
Dr. Taylor's Wellness Center, Inc.
3601 Algonquin Road
Suite 801
Rolling Meadows, IL 60008
(847) 222-1192

Pieter Van Heule, D.C.
522 Poplar Drive
Wilmette, IL 60091
(847) 251-0044

Scott Varley, D.C.
1750 Grand Stand Place
Elgin, IL 60123
(847) 888-3131

Tom Voitas, D.C.
2835 N. Sheffield Avenue
Chicago, IL 60657
(773) 880-2316

Colon Therapy

Berlina R. Baker
Chicago
(773) 994-6323

Alyce Sorokie
Chicago
(773) 868-4062

Counseling

Robert Ahrens, L.C.S.W.
Evanston
(847) 328-7174
Individual, group, and couple counseling; also counseling for men dealing with infertility issues.

Sylvia Babbin, Ph.D.
Chicago
(312) 649-5730
Individual, couple, and family counseling.

Yvonne Christman, D.Sc., R.H.D., M.H.D., C.C.H.T.
Bloomingdale
(630) 924-8947
Hypnotherapy and counseling.

Louise Dimiceli-Mitran, MT-BC
Chicago
(773) 604-5200
Guided imagery and music therapy.

David H. Johnson, L.C.S.W.
Chicago/Evanston
(847) 475-3017
Individual and couple counseling.

Bruce Koff, M.S.W.
Chicago
(773) 880-1314
Gay, lesbian, and group counseling, plus counseling for survivors of violence and abuse.

Roberta Lewis
Chicago/Evanston
(773) 761-6300
Hypnotherapy, guided holistic counseling, shamanic energetic healing, and expressive arts therapy.

David Lindgren, M.A.
Chicago/Evanston
(773) 252-7538
Individual and couple counseling, family counseling with adolescents, and group counseling for men.

Susan Lipschutz, M.S.W.
Chicago
(773) 880-2404
Psychospiritual healing and shamanic journey.

Bob Mark, Ph.D.
Evanston
(847) 864-2811
Clinical psychologist specializing in men's counseling.

Bill Martin, M.S.W., L.C.S.W.
Chicago
(773) 296-8410
Individual, couple, and family counseling.

Buddy S. Portugal, M.S.W., L.C.S.W.
Skokie
(847) 470-1420
Individual, couple, and family counseling, plus men's counseling.

Linda Randle, M.E.D., L.C.P.C.
Chicago
(773) 477-0068
Individual and couple counseling.

Gary Walls, Ph.D.
Chicago/Northfield
(312) 828-9109
Clinical psychologist specializing in individual, couple, and family counseling.

Dentists
All of these practitioners are licensed general dentists.

Gary Alberts, D.D.S., and Seymour L. Gottlieb, D.D.S.
821 Sunset Ridge Road
Northbrook, IL 60062
(847) 272-7874

Marcia Basciano, D.D.S.
2932 Finley Road
Downers Grove, IL 60515
(630) 629-6299

Blaine Cusack, D.D.S.
475 W. 55th Street
LaGrange, IL 60525
(708) 482-0300

Daniel Dieska, D.D.S.
17726-A Oak Park Avenue
Tinley Park, IL 60477
(708) 429-4700

Edwin T. Jach, D.D.S.
19900 Governors Drive
Olympia Fields, IL 60461
(708) 748-4222

Claudio Levato, D.D.S.
183 S. Bloomingdale Road
Suite 200
Bloomingdale, IL 60108
(630) 529-2522

Taf Paulson, D.D.S.
233 E. Erie Street
Suite 816
Chicago, IL 60611
(312) 944-7444

Tereau Pearson, D.M.D.
6355 N. Broadway
 Suite 31
Chicago, IL 60626
(773) 274-4864

Marianne Schaefer, D.D.S.
4801 W. Peterson Avenue
Chicago, IL 60646
11141 S. Kedzie Avenue
Chicago, IL 60655
(773) 777-8300

Rita Schneemilch, D.D.S.
416 E. Ogden Avenue
Hinsdale, IL 60521
(630) 654-0191

Harvey I. Wolf, D.D.S.,
M.P.H.
1410 S. Barrington Road
Suite 3
Barrington, IL 60010
(847) 382-5511

Ieva K. Wright, D.D.S.
333 N. Michigan Avenue
Suite 2900
Chicago, IL 60601
(312) 236-3226

Energy Field Work
Jay Arovas
Chicago
(773) 472-1373
Hawaiian energetics.

John Chamans
Morton Grove
(847) 965-5695
Hawaiian energetics.

Yvonne Christman
Bloomingdale
(630) 924-8947
Crystal healing, Rohun therapy, and Reiki.

Julie Fedeli
Chicago
(773) 404-0114

Carla Gorsky
Green Oaks/Libertyville
(847) 367-8842

Marianna Jenkins
Homewood
(708) 758-7063
Chakra balancing, light puncture therapy, and Reiki.

Suzanne Mitchem, R.N.
Tinley Park
(708) 429-9666
Pranic healing, Rohun therapy, and Reiki.

Michael Soto
Chicago
(773) 784-3112
Reiki.

Ed Kaleolani Spencer, R.N.
Chicago
(773) 275-9940
Hawaiian energetics.

Holly Whedbee
Chicago
(773) 275-9940
Hawaiian energetics.

Feng Shui

Paula M. Lund and Gunn Hollingsworth
Chicago
(773) 761-0799

Annette McCarthy
Chicago
(773) 282-8546

Jacqui Neurauger
Palatine
(847) 359-6391

Flower Essence Therapy

Liz McCormick
Oak Park
(708) 383-7438

Holistic Physicians

Alan F. Bain, D.O.
104 S. Michigan Avenue
Chicago, IL 60603
(312) 236-7010
Allergy elimination, internal medicine, and acupuncture.

Mary S. Blanks, M.D.
10725 S. Western Avenue
Chicago, IL 60643
(773) 233-6500
Obstetrics and gynecology.

Susan K. Busse, M.D.
Busse Wellness Center
909 E. Palatine Road
Suite F
Palatine, IL 60067
(847) 776-2111
Family practice; specialist in the treatment of lyme disease.

Bruno Cortis, M.D., F.A.C.C.
7605 1/2 W. North Avenue
River Forest, IL 60305
(708) 366-7200
Internal medicine and cardiology.

Marco A. De La Cruz, M.D.
Whole Health Options
5310 N. Sheridan Road
Chicago, IL 60640
(773) 784-3333
606 Potter Road
Des Plaines, IL 60016
(847) 803-6400
Family practice.

Richard A. Feely, D.O.
American WholeHealth
150 E. Huron, Suite 1100
Chicago, IL 60611
(312) 266-8565
20303 S. Crawford Avenue,
Suite 140
Olympia Fields, IL 60461
(708) 747-8565
Osteopathic manipulative medicine, acupuncture, and Chinese herbal medicine.

Ann L. Hammon, M.D.
(773) 296-2195
Psychiatry.

Pauline Harding, M.D.
27 W. 281 Geneva Road
Suite D
Winfield, IL 60190
(630) 653-9900
Family practice.

Terrill K. Haws, D.O.
Arlington Longevity
Institute
121 S. Wilke Road
Suite 111
Arlington Heights, IL 60005
(847) 577-9451
Family practice.

Thomas Hesselink, M.D.
888 S. Edgelawn Drive
Suite 1743
Aurora, IL 60506
(630) 844-0011
Preventive medicine.

Robert F. Kidd, M.D.
4309 Medical Center Drive
McHenry, IL 60050
(815) 344-0020
Orthopedic medicine and osteopathic manipulation.

Ming Te Lin, M.D.
3235 Vollmer Road
Flossmoor, IL 60422
(708) 957-7937
Allergy elimination, immunology, homeopathy, and pediatrics.

Charles Lowe, M.D.
55 E. Washington Street
Suite 1809
Chicago, IL 60602
(312) 782-0487
1140 Lake Street, Suite 402
Oak Park, IL 60301
(708) 848-0330
Internal medicine and acupuncture.

Ruth Martens, M.D.
1913 Gladstone Drive
Wheaton, IL 60187
(630) 668-5595
Classical homeopathy.

Mary Meengs, M.D.
1953-C N. Clybourn Avenue

Chicago, IL 60614
(773) 348-1414
Family practice.

Joseph Mercola, D.O.
Optimal Wellness Center
1443 W. Schaumburg Road
Schaumburg, IL 60194
(847) 985-1777
Specializing in allergy elimination.

David Moore, D.O.
TRIAD Health Practice
Illinois Masonic Medical Center
938 W. Nelson Street
Third Floor
Chicago, IL 60657
(773) 296-8499
Internal medicine.

Andrea Rentea, M.D., and Ross Rentea, M.D.
3525 W. Peterson Avenue
Suite 611
Chicago, IL 60659
(773) 583-7793
Family practice.

Dane J. Shepherd, D.O.
55 E. Washington
Suite 1630
Chicago, IL 60602
(312) 782-9153
Osteopathy, homeopathy, nutritional counseling, and acupuncture.

Thomas Stone, M.D.
1811 Hicks Road
Rolling Meadows, IL 60008
(847) 934-1100
Environmental medicine, orthomolecular medicine, homeopathy, and psychiatry.

Howard Wolin, M.D.
1515 Sheridan Road, Suite 25
Wilmette, IL 60091
(847) 256-9030
Psychiatrist.

David J. Zyeger, D.O.
REMA Medical Associates, Ltd.
150 E. Huron Street
Suite 1100
Chicago, IL 60611
(312) 951-1117
Osteopathic manipulation, family practice, and nutritional medicine.

Insurance

Alliance for Natural Health
P.O. Box 4035
Hammond, IN 46324
(888) 773-7556
As of the writing of this book, insurance plans that offer a comprehensive

package for alternative health care are almost nonexistent, especially for the Chicago area. The Natural Health Plan offered by Alliance for Natural Health is the only insurance plan in the area that offers coverage of several alternative healing therapies including acupuncture, alternative birthing centers and midwifery services, Ayurvedic medicine, biofeedback, massage therapy, nutritional counseling, chelation treatment, chiropractic, colon therapy, herbal medicine, homeopathic remedies, naturopathy, and Chinese medicine.

Illinois Department of Insurance
Consumers Division
100 W. Randolph Drive
Suite 15-100
Chicago, IL 62767
Some alternative therapies are covered by traditional insurance plans.

Patients who receive unreasonable denials of their health claims should write their complaints to this agency.

Meditation Instruction
The Himalayan Institute's Holistic Health Center
1505 Greenwood Road
Glenview, IL 60026
(847) 724-0300

Sivananda Yoga Vedanta Center
1246 W. Bryn Mawr Avenue
Chicago, IL 60660
(773) 878-7771

The Temple of Kriya Yoga
2414 N. Kedzie Avenue
Chicago, IL 60647
(773) 342-4600

Patrick Tully
Chicago
(773) 989-2112

Sohan Annette Wilkerson
Chicago
(773) 381-9606

Midwifery
Chicago Community Midwives
2112 W. Roscoe Street
Chicago, IL 60618
(773) 327-7155

New Life Midwifery Services
4740 N. Lincoln Avenue

Second Floor
Chicago, IL 60625
(773) 334-6080

Naprapaths

Ulf Henricsson, D.N.
101 W. Grand Avenue
Suite 402
Chicago, IL 60610
(312) 661-0660

Sheila Leidy, D.N.
101 W. Grand Avenue
Suite 402
Chicago, IL 60610
(312) 661-0660

Elaine Stocker, D.N.
Healing Hands
4242 N. Sheridan Road
Suite 117
Chicago, IL 60613
(773) 281-7100

Naturopaths

Alvenia M. Fulton, N.D.
Fultonia Health and Fasting Institute
1953 W. 63rd Street
Chicago, IL 60636
(773) 436-6770

Hugh Jenkins, N.D.
2148 W. 95th Street
Chicago, IL 60643
(773) 445-6800

Julie Martin, N.D.
273 Market Square, Suite 14
Lake Forest, IL 60045
(847) 735-9142

Nutritional Counseling

Janet Angel, Ph.D.
Wheeling
(847) 541-8229

Darryl Brayboy
Winnetka
(847) 441-6157
Macrobiotic counseling.

Marianna Jenkins
Chicago Heights
(708) 758-7063

Barbara Kravets
Chicago, North/Northwest, and Western suburbs
(847) 432-0225

Leslie Limberg
Chicago
(773) 296-6700
(312) 409-0046

Bonnie Minsky
Northbrook
(847) 498-3422

Pfeiffer Treatment Center
1804 Centre Point Drive
Naperville, IL 60563
(630) 505-0494

Judith Reninger
Wheaton
(630) 653-2272

Alyce Sorokie
Chicago
(773) 868-4062

Pet Care
Animas
320 E. Neville Drive
Grayslake, IL 60030
(847) 223-5593
Hours   Monday through Friday 9:00 A.M. to 5:00 P.M.; Saturday 8:30 A.M. to 1:00 P.M.; closed Sunday. Pamela Craig, D.V.M., offers holistic health care for animals at Animas, which is the derivative from the Latin word for "spirit" or "soul." Dr. Craig specializes in feline health care and has a special interest in nutritional therapy, traditional Chinese medicine, and Bach flower remedies.

Mary Baukert, D.V.M.
Skokie
(847) 729-7997
Hours: By appointment.
Acupuncture.

The Lion and the Lamb
507 E. Baltimore Street
Wilmington, IL 60481
(815) 476-7677
Hours   By appointment. This place offers pet grooming, foot massage, teeth cleaning services, plus vegetarian pet treats. Owner Peggy Johnson is a Reiki master teacher and also communicates intuitively with animals.

Paws for Thought
1821 W. Irving Park Road
Chicago, IL 60613
(773) 528-7297
Hours   Monday through Friday 12:00 P.M. to 8:00 P.M.; Saturday 11:00 A.M. to 6:00 P.M.; Sunday 12:00 to 5:00 P.M.
An alternative pet store, this place carries organic pet food, vitamins, and homeopathic remedies for animals. They also stock U.S. bleach/pesticide-free rawhides, organic cat grass, and safe biodegradable clumping litter. In addition to stocking a large inventory of all-natural products for

pets, they also provide a safe haven for homeless or abandoned cats.

Judith Rae Swanson, D.V.M.
(773) 561-4526
Hours   By appointment.
Practicing acupuncture, homeopathy, nutrition, and massage in Chicago and Lincolnwood.

Transcendental Meditation
Maharishi Vedic University
636 S. Michigan Avenue
Suite 210
Chicago, IL 60605
(312) 431-0110

2 Natural Pharmacies

My grandmother, Ma Bea, never liked taking pharmaceuticals. She believed that nature contained everything we needed to keep our bodies well and although over-the-counter drugs were useful, they merely treated the symptoms of disease rather than providing a cure. Ma Bea said that vitamins, minerals, and herbs helped the body maintain its natural state of good health and would often tell her physician that her daily dosage of natural remedies—not the regular visits she made to him—was the one and only thing that kept her body in good stead.

Once you've decided to live a more natural lifestyle, you'll also began relying less on your doctor and start assuming more responsibility for your own health and, like Ma Bea, begin looking for natural remedies rather than pharmaceuticals to cure your aches and pains. There are several resources in the area where you can get vitamins, minerals, herbs, and homeopathic remedies to help you achieve this goal.

In this chapter, I've provided you with some information about vitamin stores with personnel who are well schooled in nutritional supplements; herb shops that stock herbal remedies in root, bulk, and pill form; and places that offer Oriental herbs. I've also included information on pharmacies in the area that sell a mixture of all-natural products in addition to pharmaceutical products and over-the-counter drugs.

What isn't mentioned in this chapter is the network marketing companies, many of which promote an entire line of all-natural nutritional supplements. Mail-order houses are noticeably absent, too. I have not listed these resources because, although several of them carry effective products, my goal is to direct you to places where you can get face-to-face professional assistance.

You'll see that no natural pharmacies are listed for the South/Southwest suburbs. Unfortunately, people who live in these areas will have to travel into the city or other suburban regions to find a completely natural pharmacy.

Major Chain Stores

General Nutrition Centers (GNC)
(800) 477-4462 or refer to Appendix B
This is a successful sixty-year-old chain. They provide customers with a wide variety of health-oriented products including vitamins, minerals, sport nutritional supplements, herbal formulations, and personal care items. Some stores also carry sports equipment and athletic attire. This franchise offers discounts on a variety of nutritional products. Their two-for-the-price-of-one specials are a customer favorite. More than seventy locations in the Chicago metropolitan area.

Chicago

Back to Nature, Inc.
5098 S. Archer Avenue
Chicago, IL 60638
(773) 735-4401
Hours   Monday through Friday 10:00 A.M. to 7:00 P.M.; Saturday 9:00 A.M. to 5:00 P.M.; closed Sunday.

Back to Nature, Inc.
5898 S. Archer Avenue
Chicago, IL 60638
(773) 582-8568
Hours   Monday through Friday 10:00 A.M. to 6:00 P.M.; Saturday 9:00 A.M. to 5:00 P.M.; closed Sunday.

Back to Nature, Inc.
5556 W. Belmont Avenue
Chicago, IL 60632
(773) 481-0036
Hours   Monday through Friday 9:00 A.M. to 8:00 P.M.; Saturday 9:00 A.M. to 6:00 P.M.; Sunday 9:00 A.M. to 5:00 P.M.

Back to Nature, Inc.
3101 N. Milwaukee Avenue
Chicago, IL 60618
(773) 463-5758
Hours   Monday through Friday 9:00 A.M. to 8:00 P.M.; Saturday 9:00 A.M. to 7:00 P.M.; Sunday 9:00 A.M. to 4:00 P.M.

Back to Nature, Inc.
5627 N. Milwaukee Avenue
Chicago, IL 60646
(773) 631-1517
Hours   Monday through Friday 9:00 A.M. to 6:00 P.M.; Saturday 9:00 A.M. to 5:00 P.M.; closed Sunday.

A local vitamin store chain with five stores in the city and one located in the North/Northwest suburbs, this place offers vitamins, minerals, herbs, top-of-the-line natural remedies from Poland and Russia, and all-natural body care products from various countries in Europe. All employees speak at least one other language besides English, either Polish or Russian. The owners even publish a monthly magazine written entirely in Polish, entitled *Zdrowie, Uroda I Zycie*, which translates in English to health, beauty, and life.

Bark Lee Tong
229 W. Cermak Road
Chicago, IL 60616
(312) 225-1988
Hours   Sunday through Saturday 9:00 A.M. to 6:00 P.M.
The oldest herb shop in Chinatown, this store is more than fifty-five years old and offers a variety of Chinese herbal medicines including all-natural teas, plus Chinese herbs in bulk, root, leaf, and pill form. They also sell personal care items imported from China.

Better Health, Inc.
2323 W. Devon Avenue, Suite 202
Chicago, IL 60659
(773) 761-0107
Hours   Monday through Saturday 11:00 A.M. to 7:00 P.M.; closed Sunday.
Open to the public, this manufacturer of homeopathic single remedies has a retail outlet and is an excellent place for people to learn about homeopathy. In addition to single remedies, they also make an herbal hair tonic that stimulates hair growth, plus herbal and homeopathic formulas designed especially for men.

Broadway Vitamins
3321 N. Broadway
Chicago, IL 60657
(773) 404-9000
Hours   Monday through Friday 11:00 A.M. to 7:00 P.M.; Saturday 10:00 A.M. to 6:00 P.M.; Sunday 12:00 P.M. to 5:00 P.M.
Best known for its everyday low pricing, this storefront stocks top-of-the-line vitamins, minerals, herbs, and a small selection of all-natural health and beauty items.

Cosmopolitan Natural Pharmacy
754 N. Clark Street
Chicago, IL 60610
(312) 787-2152
Hours   Monday through Saturday 7:00 A.M. to 10:00 P.M.; closed Sunday.
This dispensary offers pharmaceuticals as well as Chinese and Western herbal preparations and extracts. They also stock vitamins, minerals, homeopathic remedies, essential oils, aromatherapy supplies, sports nutritional products, and all-natural body care items. One of the owners has a background in homeopathy and uses this knowledge to assist customers.

Dr. Michael's Herbs, Inc.
5109 N. Western Avenue
Chicago, IL 60625
(773) 271-7738
Hours   Monday through Saturday 8:00 A.M. to 6:00 P.M.; closed Sunday.
The largest herb store in the Chicago area, this place was founded in 1928 by a naturopath from Poland, the late Dr. Michael Michaels. Today, this shop supplies several of the health food stores in the city as well as markets across the country with various herbal formulations. However, in their retail shop, they stock five hundred different herbs from around the world in bark, root, powder, cut, extract, and capsule form, plus vitamins and homeopathic remedies. Personnel at the store speak English, Polish, Russian, and Spanish. Customers can also purchase products via catalog.

Great Earth Vitamin Store
2810 N. Clark Street
Chicago, IL 60657

(773) 281-1211
Hours   Monday through Friday 10:00 A.M. to 8:00 P.M.; Saturday 10:00 A.M. to 6:00 P.M.; Sunday 11:00 A.M. to 6:00 P.M.
Another national chain, this store is an excellent place to shop for body-building supplements. They also carry vitamins, herbs, homeopathic remedies, and a small selection of body care items. Their preferred customer program offers its members savings of about 15 percent on various nutritional supplements.

IMARC Pharmacy
938 W. Nelson Street
Chicago, IL 60657
(773) 296-8444
Hours   Monday and Wednesday 10:00 A.M. to 7:00 P.M.; Tuesday and Thursday 9:00 A.M. to 5:00 P.M.; Friday 9:00 A.M. to 4:00 P.M.; closed Saturday and Sunday.
Located on the campus of Illinois Masonic Medical Center and in the same building as the hospital's holistic health clinic, Strong Spirit Wellness Center, this dispensary carries vitamins, minerals, herbs, and homeopathic remedies as well as pharmaceuticals.

Merz Apothecary
4716 N. Lincoln Avenue
Chicago, IL 60625
(773) 989-0900
Hours   Monday through Saturday 9:00 A.M. to 6:00 P.M.; closed Sunday.
This 123-year-old natural pharmacy has been in its present location for more than twenty years and resembles an old-world apothecary. The types of services offered here are also reminiscent of the kind of attention customers receive in traditional European pharmacies. The pharmacists are well versed in homeopathic medicine, herbal medicine, and flower

essences. In addition to a plethora of all-natural remedies, this place also carries a wide selection of European body care products and cosmetics, most of which are plant-based and organic.

Sae Khwang Herbs
3647 W. Lawrence Avenue
Chicago, IL 60625
(773) 539-8733
Hours   Monday through Saturday 10:00 A.M. to 7:00 P.M.; closed Sunday.
A great place to shop for Oriental herbs, this spot stocks herbal remedies in extract, capsule, and bulk form.

Solomon-Cooper Drugs, Inc.
1051 N. Rush Street
Chicago, IL 60611
(312) 944-3739
Hours   Monday through Friday 8:00 A.M. to 8:00 P.M.; Saturday 9:00 A.M. to 6:00 P.M.; Sunday 9:00 A.M. to 5:00 P.M.
This store is over fifty years old and stocks a large selection of vitamins, minerals, herbs, and homeopathic remedies in addition to pharmaceuticals and over-the-counter medicines. Like many of the natural pharmacies in town, this place has a licensed nutritionist on staff who assists customers with their selection of products.

Soolim Limited
2747 W. Lawrence Avenue
Chicago, IL 60625
(773) 728-6266
Hours   Monday through Friday 9:30 A.M. to 5:30 P.M.; Saturday 10:00 A.M. to 5:00 P.M.; closed Sunday.
This place offers a variety of Chinese herbal formulations, bulk herbs, and ginseng products. It also manufactures Oriental herbs for several health food stores across the country.

North/Northwest Suburbs

Back to Nature, Inc.
269 Dundee Road
Wheeling, IL 60090
(847) 520-5285
Hours   Monday through Friday 10:00 A.M. to 6:30 P.M.; Saturday 10:00 A.M. to 6:00 A.M.
See Chicago listing for details.

Walsh Homeopathics
2116 1/2 Central Street
Evanston, IL 60201
(847) 864-1600
Hours   Monday through Saturday 10:00 A.M. to 6:00 A.M.; closed Sunday.
This dispensary offers homeopathic and herbal remedies as well as homeopathic formulations for animals. They also carry Bach flower remedies, organic essential oils, all-natural body care products, and food-grown vitamins and minerals. In addition to natural health remedies, they stock supplies to help their customers maintain a healthy home environment such as air filters, full-spectrum light bulbs, and feng shui supplies. Other offerings include an alternative practitioner referral service and a toll-free number (1-800-992-5747) for customers who want to order products by phone.

Western Suburbs

Larrabee Herbs
7230 W. North Avenue
Elmwood Park, IL 60707
(708) 453-7898
Hours Monday, Tuesday, and Wednesday 9:30 A.M. to 6:00 P.M.; Thursday and Friday 9:30 A.M. to 8:00 P.M.; Saturday 9:30 A.M. to 5:00 P.M.; closed Sunday.

Another great place to shop for Western herbs, this 125-year-old natural pharmacy was originally based in Chicago and currently bears the name of its former address in the city on Larrabee Street. This pharmacy stocks more than 450 dry herbs, several of which come in capsule and tea form. They also carry vitamins, minerals, homeopathic products, aromatherapy items, and Bach flower remedies. All the staff members here are licensed nutritionists.

3 Natural Food Shopping

"You are what you eat," I remember my mother saying as she scooped a spoonful of vegetables I didn't like onto my plate. For a long time I resented her for always urging me to eat okra, asparagus, and broccoli, but, since I've grown older, I now realize how important it is to eat fresh foods, especially fruits and vegetables, and am finally grateful for my mother's constant prodding.

When I approached my thirties, I noticed the extent to which different foods affected my body. I discovered that eating Caesar salad with a soy-based dressing made me feel more vibrant and alive, while eating too many beef and dairy products made my body feel heavy and lethargic. I also began to observe how different foods and beverages affected my emotions. Drinking chamomile tea, for example, really seemed to soothe me, while sipping a cup of coffee or a carbonated soda caused my heart to palpitate. That's when I concluded that foods and beverages not only had a tremendous affect on my body, but also on my mind and spirit.

If you're like me and have discovered that food plays a major role in the overall quality of your life, you may want to make some changes in your diet. Fortunately, you live in a city that has plenty of health food stores and natural food markets that carry plenty of products to help you make the transition.

When you walk into one of these stores, you may be a little overwhelmed by the various brands of merchandise on the shelves. Now that people are growing more concerned about their health, many more food manufacturers have joined the heart-healthy bandwagon and the number of healthy food items available has exploded. But don't let the different brand names intimidate you. What's great about these stores is that the personnel are very familiar with the products and are willing to help you sift through them. Some staff members are even trained nutritional counselors or alternative therapists and can offer expert advice regarding your product selection.

If you don't need personal assistance right away, you'll find information regarding some of these products in the store's information center or in a rack displayed near the book section. As you browse the aisles, however, you'll discover that although you may not recognize the brand names, the products themselves may seem strangely familiar. "There's a counterpart for almost anything you can find in your grocery store at the health food store," says Gina Geslewitz, editor of *Health Food Business* magazine. "You'll find Pop-Tarts, SpaghettiOs, and snack crackers in a conventional grocery store, but when you visit a natural food store, you'll find the healthier version of that same kind of product made by manufacturers like Health Valley or Tree of Life." The big difference is that the healthier versions don't contain ingredients that are detrimental to your health.

According to Al Powers, owner of the local chain The Fruitful Yield and Here's Health stores, and president of a cooperative network of health food stores called The Natural Way, the health food store acts as a buying agent for the consumer. "Customers should be able to walk into a health food store and be assured that the products they just purchased are good for them," Powers says.

The best health food stores in town have a list of quality standards that food manufacturers must meet before their products can be sold to customers. These standards specify the type of products the store carries on its shelves and usually include only food that is free of artificial sweeteners, colors, artificial flavors, and preservatives; meat, poultry, and seafood products that are free of added growth hormones, antibiotics, nitrates, and other chemicals; grains that have not been bleached or bromated; and household and personal care items that are both earth-friendly and haven't been tested on animals.

In addition to selling food, these stores also stock a line of nutritional products including vitamins, minerals, herbs, and homeopathic remedies. Some stores even carry essential oils and Bach flower essences.

Beyond all the items that these stores offer for sale, some natural food stores are regarded as a meeting place—a place for the health-conscious crowd to hang out. The larger natural food markets usually have a prepared food department and provide a dining area where customers can eat, sit, and chat. Several stores in the city have organic juice bars and delis in the building where chefs whip up fresh fruit and vegetable juices, protein drinks, and wheat-grass shots or prepare vegetarian and vegan meals while customers wait.

In almost all of these stores, there's a book section where customers can browse through books and magazines about alternative health therapies and different topics regarding healthy living.

What isn't listed in this chapter are grocery stores like Dominick's Fresh Stores, Jewel Food Stores, Mr. G Co-op, and the Hyde Park Co-op because they carry a small selection of organic produce and nutritional supplements and don't offer the kind of product expertise you'll find at the following health food stores. The Sunset Food Market in Northbrook is mentioned because its health food department is the size of a veritable health food store. This chain's other outlets have been omitted because their selection of natural food products is much smaller.

Farmer's markets are not mentioned even though these outdoor venues have always provided customers with a wide selection of fresh fruits and vegetables and are now offering a larger selection of organic produce. Retail cooperatives are not listed because, although they have historically been a good source for natural food products, most of them have been forced to place less emphasis on natural foods to stay competitive in the marketplace.

The stores that are listed in this section are some of the best health food stores in the Chicago metropolitan area. They are mentioned because of the length of time they've been in business, which means the personnel at these stores really know their stuff. They are also listed for the unique quality of their store and the high degree of service they give their customers, most of which goes beyond just providing their customers with healthy food items. The stores that are listed also offer an added service of some kind, ranging from nutritional counseling (sometimes fee-free) to vegetarian cooking classes. After visiting just a few of the stores listed in this chapter, you'll see just how much support you have in your quest to live a more healthy and vibrant life.

Chicago

All the Best Nutrition
3008 W. Devon Avenue
Chicago, IL 60659
(773) 274-9478
Hours   Monday through Thursday 10:00 A.M. to 6:30 P.M.; Friday 10:00 A.M. to 6:00 P.M.; Saturday 10:00 A.M. to 5:00 P.M.; Sunday 11:00 A.M. to 4:00 P.M.
A health food emporium that focuses mainly on nutritional supplements, this store carries a wide variety of vitamins including Kosher vitamins, top-of-the-line herbs, minerals, and

homeopathic remedies. They also carry organic packaged and frozen foods, whole grains, and body care products.

Better Living Health Food Store
8338 S. Ashland Avenue
Chicago, IL 60620
(773) 779-3339
Hours   Monday through Friday 10:00 A.M. to 7:00 P.M.; Saturday 9:00 A.M. to 6:00 P.M.; closed Sunday.
This place lives up to its name by providing a wide range of products to help people live a healthier life. Customers can choose from a variety of herbs, vitamins, minerals, and all-natural medicinal teas. There's also a frozen food section with an array of meat alternatives. The beauty center is well stocked with an assortment of all-natural body care items, including hair-care supplies.

Bonne Santé
1457 E. 53rd Street
Chicago, IL 60615
(773) 667-5700
Hours   Monday through Friday 9:30 A.M. to 7:00 P.M.; Saturday 9:30 A.M. to 6:00 P.M.; Sunday 11:00 A.M. to 5:00 P.M.
Bonne Santé, a French expression meaning "good health," contains a well-stocked macrobiotic section. Other offerings include a wide selection of herbs, vitamins, homeopathic remedies, organic packaged goods, and bulk grains and beans. Like other stores, it also has an organic juice bar.

Earth and Sea
11122 S. Western Avenue
Chicago, IL 60643
(773) 881-0075
Hours   Monday through Friday 10:00 A.M. to 6:00 P.M.; Saturday 10:00 A.M. to 5:00 P.M.; closed Sunday.
The owner of this strip-mall spot, Pat Boldt, is the sister of

Robert J. Corr and sells his soft drink, Corr's Natural Soda, at her store for just fifty cents a can. In addition to offering an assortment of natural soft drinks, she also carries a variety of vitamins, minerals, herbs, and organic packaged goods.

Elnora's Health Unlimited
10844 S. Halsted Street
Chicago, IL 60628
(773) 995-0162
Hours   Monday through Saturday 9:00 A.M. to 8:00 P.M.; closed Sunday.
A small but well-supplied health food store, Elnora's has a deli and organic juice bar where the chef prepares fresh vegetarian meals daily. Homemade pastries made with all-natural ingredients are a favorite. There's also a wide selection of herbs and herbal teas.

Here's Health Stores, Inc.
22 W. Maple Avenue
Chicago, IL 60610
(312) 397-1501
Hours   Monday through Friday 7:30 A.M. to 7:30 P.M.;   Saturday 8:00 A.M. to 5:30 P.M.;   Sunday 10:00 A.M. to 5:30 P.M.
This chain has been around for more than twenty years and offers an extensive inventory of sports nutrition products as well as vitamins, minerals, herbs, organic packaged goods, and organic produce. The Chicago store has a deli and organic juice bar where patrons can enjoy vegetarian or heart-healthy entrées.

Hy-Tek
3304 W. 87th Street
Chicago, IL 60652
(773) 436-3000
Hours   Monday through Thursday 9:00 A.M. to 9:00 P.M.; Friday and Saturday 10:00 A.M. to 6:00 P.M.; closed Sunday.

In addition to providing their customers with high quality natural food products, this store offers vitamins, herbs, and minerals. A coffee-house-style sitting area provides a cozy niche for customers to read books about health or sip their favorite drinks purchased from the organic juice bar. Besides the friendly, professional service that's offered by staff members, a computer with information on nutritional products is on hand and can be used by customers to assist them with nutritional product selection.

It's Natural
324 N. Michigan Avenue
Chicago, IL 60601
(312) 269-0618
Hours   Monday through Friday 8:00 A.M. to 6:00 P.M. (winter hours); Monday through Friday 8:00 A.M. to 7:00 P.M. (summer hours); Saturday 10:00 A.M. to 6:00 P.M.; Sunday 10:00 A.M. to 4:00 P.M. (all seasons).
The Magnificent Mile's most popular health food store and juice bar, It's Natural is one of the few places downtown where you can purchase a quick, heart-healthy meal. This store offers ready-to-eat salads and sandwiches that can be eaten on the run or enjoyed on the premises. There's also a wide selection of nutritional supplements and health and beauty items.

Leo Naturals
3242 W. Foster Avenue
Chicago, IL 60625
(773) 267-0808
Hours   Monday through Saturday 10:00 A.M. to 7:00 P.M.; closed Sunday.
This thirty-something-year-old store is an excellent resource for Chinese medicine and herbs. It carries acupuncture needles, moxa (dried mugwort used by some acupuncturists), oriental herbs, Chinese patent pills, herbal teas, and organic

packaged goods. An acupuncturist on staff offers consultations and treatments to customers by appointment only.

Life Spring
3178 N. Clark Street
Chicago, IL 60657
(773) 327-1023
Hours   Monday through Friday 9:30 A.M. to 7:30 P.M.; Saturday 9:30 A.M. to 6:00 P.M.; Sunday 1:00 P.M. to 5:00 P.M.
A small retail outlet packed with all kinds of health-related items, this store and organic juice bar has been serving Northside residents for more than twenty years. They carry wall-to-wall nutritional supplements, including sports nutrition supplements, which is their specialty. They also serve frozen yogurt.

The Life Store
1639 E. 87th Street
Chicago, IL 60617
(773) 731-2530
Hours   Monday through Saturday 10:00 A.M. to 6:30 P.M.; closed Sunday.
This family-owned and -operated store has been in business for more than twenty years and stocks a variety of health food products. There's a large selection of nutritional supplements as well as herbal teas, including medicinals. There's also a well-stocked refrigerated section with a variety of meat alternatives.

Morse Avenue Natural Foods
1527 W. Morse Avenue
Chicago, IL 60626
(773) 743-7190
Hours   Monday through Friday 11:00 A.M. to 7:00 P.M.; Saturday 10:00 A.M. to 6:00 P.M.; Sunday 12:00 P.M. to 5:00 P.M.
A full-service health food and vitamin shop complete with an organic produce section, this store has a deli on the second

floor that serves up a variety of vegetarian foods including chili, stir-fry dishes, soups, and baked goods.

The Natural Food Connection
8517 S. State Street
Chicago, IL 60619
(773) 846-2661
Hours   Monday through Wednesday 9:00 A.M. to 5:30 P.M.; Thursday 9:00 A.M. to 7:00 P.M.; Friday 9:00 A.M. to 1:00 P.M.; closed Saturday and Sunday.
Located in the Seven Day Adventists' Lake Region Conference Building, this store offers vitamins, herbs, and minerals like other stores in the city, but what sets it apart from the rest is its vast selection of vegetarian foods, especially meat alternatives. This store carries everything from vegetarian dinner roast to Wham (the soy version of ham). They even sell sliced lunch meat made from vegetable protein.

A Natural Harvest
7122 S. Jeffery Boulevard
Chicago, IL 60649
(773) 363-3939
Hours   Monday through Friday 10:00 A.M. to 7:00 P.M.; Saturday 10:00 A.M. to 6:30 P.M.; closed Sunday.
This strip-mall shopping spot not only carries a variety of healthy snack foods, they also have a large selection of herbal teas, vitamins, herbs, and organic packaged goods. There's a deli and organic juice bar in the rear of the store where patrons can buy a variety of vegetarian meals including meatless burgers and tacos made from vegetable protein.

New Approach Health Foods
641 E. 47th Street
Chicago, IL 60653
(773) 373-6900
Hours   Monday through Saturday 9:00 A.M. to 8:00 P.M.;

closed Sunday.

This outlet is more than a health food store, it's a neighborhood meeting place. On the last Saturday of each month, the store turns into an entertainment center of sorts where local artists read poetry, play music, and even dance. In keeping with its health food store theme, however, it offers customers an assortment of vitamins, minerals, herbs, and natural food products, as well as freshly prepared vegetarian and heart-healthy meals from an adjoining restaurant and an organic juice bar.

Pass Health Foods
3250 W. 55th Street
Chicago, IL 60632
(773) 776-1894
Hours   Monday through Saturday 9:00 A.M. to 6:00 P.M.; closed Sunday.

The place to shop for herbal teas, this store carries more than one hundred different blends, including medicinals. They also stock top-of-the-line nutritional supplements and organic packaged goods.

Sherwyn's Health Food Shops, Inc.
645 W. Diversey Avenue
Chicago, IL 60614
(773) 477-1934
Hours   Monday through Friday 9:00 A.M. to 8:00 P.M.; Saturday 9:00 A.M. to 7:00 P.M.; Sunday 11:00 A.M. to 6:00 P.M.

A Chicago favorite, this health food store has a large selection of nearly everything health related, especially vitamins, minerals, herbs, and organic produce. It's a great resource for people with food allergies or diabetes since the products on the shelves are free of both white flour and sugar. The organic juice bar is one of the largest in the city and features a menu of more than forty freshly prepared fruit and vegetable juices, including kamut grass and ginseng mixes. Sherwyn's also has a well-stocked health and beauty section with a professional cosmetologist on staff to assist customers with their choice of cruelty-free cosmetics and body care products.

Southtown Health Foods
2100 W. 95th Street
Chicago, IL 60643
(773) 233-1856
Hours   Monday through Saturday 9:30 A.M. to 5:30 P.M.; Thursday 9:30 A.M. to 8:00 P.M.; closed Sunday.
This fifty-five-year-old natural food store and organic juice bar stocks a wide variety of organic meats from New York strip steaks to lamb chops. In addition to having one of the largest organic meat departments in the Chicago area, they also offer a wide selection of vitamins, herbs, homeopathic remedies, organic packaged goods, and organic produce.

Sunflower Seed
5210 S. Harper Avenue
Chicago, IL 60615
(773) 363-1600
Hours   Monday through Saturday 10:00 A.M. to 6:00 P.M.; closed Sunday.
A small health food store located on the second level of Harper Court in Hyde Park, this place offers everything from ear candles to herbs. They have a wide selection of vitamins, minerals, tinctures, and homeopathic remedies. And, like in many of these stores, there's also an organic juice bar.

True Nature Foods
6034 N. Broadway Avenue
Chicago, IL 60660
(773) 465-6400
Hours   Monday through Saturday 10:00 A.M. to 7:00 P.M.; Sunday 12:00 P.M. to 5:00 P.M.
The place to shop for bulk foods, this place also carries an array of vitamins, minerals, and herbal products.

Whole Foods Market
1000 W. North Avenue
Chicago, IL 60622
(312) 587-0648
Hours   Monday through Sunday 8:00 A.M. to 10:00 P.M. (winter hours); Monday through Sunday 8:00 A.M. to 11:00 P.M. (summer hours).

Whole Foods Market
3300 N. Ashland Avenue
Chicago, IL 60657
(773) 244-4200
Hours   Monday through Sunday 8:00 A.M. to 10:00 P.M.

A health food mega-market, Whole Foods offers a vast selection of natural foods plus items that you'd find in some conventional grocery stores like seafood, beer, wine, cheese, baked goods, and meat, except the products sold here are mostly 100 percent organic. There are, however, other sections that you won't find at your neighborhood market, like the macrobiotic section and a nutritional center with several brands of vitamins, minerals, herbs, and homeopathic remedies, not to mention a bulk section with a variety of dry goods, oils, nut butters, herbs, and spices. Shoppers can also purchase corn-, wheat-, and dairy-free products, as well as meatless, low-sugar, and low-fat foods from off the shelves or ready-to-eat from the prepared foods department. There's also a wide range of organic and high-quality, conventionally grown produce. The North Avenue store even has a restaurant, eden, the natural bistro, situated on the second floor with a menu of vegan, vegetarian, and heart-healthy entrées.

North/Northwest Suburbs

Annapurna Herb Shop
814 Dempster Street
Evanston, IL 60202
(847) 869-4609
Hours Monday, Tuesday, Wednesday, Friday, and Saturday 10:00 A.M. to 6:00 P.M.; Thursday 10:00 A.M. to 8:00 P.M.; closed Sunday.
The Chicago area's premier source for Ayurvedic products and one of the newest stores in town, this shop, which occupies two rooms in a building that used to be a bookstore, offers everything from spices used in Ayurvedic cooking to books on Ayurvedic medicine and yoga. One side of the store is a natural pharmacy containing herbs, botanical oils, flower essences, and all-natural cosmetics. The other side consists of an array of natural food products and a book section.

Blue Sky Market
39 Huntington Lane
Wheeling, IL 60090
(847) 541-8118
Hours Monday through Friday 9:00 A.M. to 8:00 P.M.; Saturday 9:00 A.M. to 7:00 P.M.; Sunday 9:00 A.M. to 5:00 P.M.
The main thing that differentiates this health food store from others in the Chicago area is the expertise of its owner. Dr. Janet M. Angel, a nutritional biochemist, research scientist, and psychologist, offers a variety of health food products, including wheat- and dairy-free foods, as well as nutritional counseling services right in her store. Some of the consulting services she provides include nutritional and subtle energy field analyses; parasite and osteoporosis risk testing; stress counseling; and relaxation, meditation, and guided-imagery sessions.

Crystal Lake Health Food Store
25 E. Crystal Lake Avenue
Crystal Lake, IL 60014
(815) 459-7942
Hours   Monday, Tuesday, Wednesday, and Friday 9:00 A.M. to 6:00 P.M.; Thursday 9:00 A.M. to 7:00 P.M.; Saturday 9:00 A.M. to 5:00 P.M.; closed Sunday.

Shoppers will find herbs in almost every variation at this health food store and can purchase them in bulk, capsule, and liquid form. There are also several brands of nutritional supplements and homeopathic remedies as well as wheat-, gluten-, and dairy-free products, plus home brewing supplies for making beer and wine.

Fruitful Yield
Schaumburg Marketplace
175 W. Gold Road
Schaumburg, IL 60194
(847) 882-2999
Hours   Monday through Friday 9:30 A.M. to 8:30 P.M.; Saturday 9:00 A.M. to 6:00 P.M.; Sunday 10:00 A.M. to 5:00 P.M.

Fruitful Yield
5005 Oakton Street
Skokie, IL 60077
(847) 679-8882
Hours   Monday 10:00 A.M. to 7:00 P.M.; Tuesday, Wednesday, and Friday 10:00 A.M. to 6:00 P.M.; Thursday 10:00 A.M. to 8:00 P.M.; Saturday 10:00 A.M. to 5:00 P.M.; closed Sunday.

Fruitful Yield may be a little bigger than most neighborhood health food stores, but the courtesy of their staff is what gives this local chain its warm mom-and-pop-shop kind of feel. All the products in this store are naturally sweetened and are free of hydrogenated oils and other artificial ingredients. The store also features milk products that are free of BGH (Bovine Growth Hormone). Depending upon the season, customers are sure to find plenty of their favorite fruits and vegetables in the organic produce section. There are also nutritionists on staff customers may consult about dietary changes. Nutritional counseling is provided at no charge.

Here's Health Stores, Inc.
704 S. Northwest Highway
Barrington, IL 60010
(847) 381-4210
Hours   Monday through Friday 9:00 A.M. to 8:00 P.M.; Saturday 9:30 A.M. to 6:00 P.M.; Sunday 12:00 P.M. to 5:00 P.M.

Here's Health Stores, Inc.
Deerbrook Mall
178 S. Waukegan Road
Deerfield, IL 60015
(847) 564-8870
Hours   Monday through Friday 9:30 A.M. to 9:00 P.M.; Saturday 9:30 A.M. to 6:00 P.M.; Sunday 11:00 A.M. to 5:00 P.M.

Here's Health Stores, Inc.
302 S. McLean Boulevard
Elgin, IL 60123
(847) 888-0100
Hours   Monday through Friday 9:30 A.M. to 6:00 P.M.; Saturday 9:30 A.M. to 6:00 P.M.; Sunday 11:00 A.M. to 5:00 P.M.
See Chicago listing for details.

Murphy's Health Foods and Juice Bar
400 N. Milwaukee Avenue
Libertyville, IL 60048
(847) 362-4664
Hours   Monday, Tuesday, Wednesday, and Friday 9:00 A.M. to 6:00 P.M.; Thursday 9:00 A.M. to 7:00 P.M.; Saturday 9:00 A.M. to 5:00 P.M.; closed Sunday.
This store has been around for twenty-seven years, but has a new location and name. Formerly Lutz's Health Food Store,

the new store, affectionately known as Murphy's, stocks a huge selection of natural vitamins, minerals, and herbal supplements. There's also plenty of food choices for people who are lactose intolerant, including non-dairy milk, cheese, sour cream, and cream cheese, plus a variety of wheat-free and gluten-free products and a juice bar. Vegetarian cooking demonstrations are held throughout the year.

Nature's Cornucopia Natural Food and Nutrition Center
1259 N. Green Street
McHenry, IL 60050
(815) 385-4500
Hours   Monday through Thursday 8:30 A.M. to 6:00 P.M.; Friday 8:30 A.M. to 7:00 P.M.; Saturday 8:30 A.M. to 5:00 P.M.; closed Sunday.
Housed in a building that was a drug store at the turn of the century, this store still has the ambiance of an old general store, except the stock they carry does not include pharmaceuticals, but some of the best nutritional products available. In addition to carrying top-of-the-line vitamins, herbs, and mineral supplements, this business of over ten years also stocks a complete line of homeopathic products and organic packaged goods. The staff consists of certified natural health professionals and licensed nutritionists who offer new customers a free forty-minute nutritional counseling session.

Nature's Cupboard
1488 Waukegan Road
Glenview, IL 60025
(847) 729-3220
Hours   Monday through Friday 10:00 A.M. to 7:00 P.M.; Saturday 9:00 A.M. to 5:30 P.M.; Sunday 12:00 P.M. to 4:00 P.M.
The Chicago area's first macrobiotic store, this place sells every macrobiotic product imaginable, from toasted sesame oil to pickled ume plums. Cooking classes are taught by a Kushi

Institute–trained teacher and organic macrobiotic lunches are prepared fresh on weekdays.

Oak Mill Natural Foods
8062 N. Milwaukee Avenue
Niles, IL 60714
(847) 825-5424
Hours   Monday, Tuesday, Wednesday, and Friday 10:00 A.M. to 6:00 P.M.; Thursday 10:00 A.M. to 8:00 P.M.; Saturday 9:30 A.M. to 5:00 P.M.; closed Sunday.
This store has been serving the Chicago area for over twenty-seven years and offers a variety of vitamins, minerals, herbs, herbal teas, homeopathic remedies, sports nutrition, organic packaged goods, and cruelty-free cosmetics.

Polson's Natural Foods
960 Main Street
Antioch, IL 60002
(847) 395-0461
Hours   Monday through Thursday 9:00 A.M. to 6:00 P.M.; Friday 9:00 A.M. to 8:00 P.M.; Saturday 9:00 A.M. to 5:00 P.M.; closed Sunday.
This seventy-year-old store is one of the oldest health food markets in the Chicago area and carries vitamins, herbs, bulk dry goods, and a wide variety of refrigerated and frozen grocery items. It's one of the few stores in town where customers can find 100 percent organic beef. They also sell juicers and water distillers.

Sun Grain Health Products
628 Grove Street
Evanston, IL 60201
(847) 328-6366
Hours   Monday through Friday 9:30 A.M. to 6:00 P.M.; Saturday 10:00 A.M. to 5:00 P.M.; closed Sunday.
Sun Grain Health Products is the Chicago area's number one

source for Birkenstock shoes, with more than one thousand pairs of the comfy shoes for sale. The store also carries vitamins, herbs, a small selection of organic packaged goods, and cruelty-free body care products.

Sunset Food Mart
1901 Cherry Lane
Northbrook, IL 60062
(847) 272-7700
This neighborhood food mart was one of the first in the Chicago area to incorporate a large natural food section into a grocery store. Their two-thousand-square-foot health food section contains vitamins, minerals, homeopathic remedies, and no-animal-testing cosmetics and organic body care products. They also have a large selection of organic packaged goods, organic refrigerated and frozen items, plus vegetarian food items. Their bulk section is one of the best in town and contains all kinds of pasta, grains, legumes, and even herbs and spices. As with most health food stores, there's also a book section. Guest speakers lecture at this place every month on some aspect of holistic health.

A Way of Life, Inc.
9359 Milwaukee Avenue
Niles, IL 60714
(847) 966-5565
Hours   Monday through Friday 10:00 A.M. to 9:00 P.M.; Saturday 9:30 A.M. to 6:00 P.M.; Sunday 12:00 P.M. to 5:00 P.M.
Shoppers will find a variety of products at this store, including vitamins, minerals, herbs, homeopathic remedies, sports nutrition products, diet products, liquid extracts, pet care products, vegetarian frozen foods, and organic packaged goods. A licensed nutritional counselor is always on the premises.

Whole Foods Market
1630 Chicago Avenue
Evanston, IL 60201
(847) 733-1600
Hours   Monday through Sunday 8:00 A.M. to 9:00 P.M.

Whole Foods Market
1331 N. Rand Road
Palatine, IL 60067
(847) 776-8080
Hours   Monday through Saturday 8:00 A.M. to 9:00 P.M.; Sunday 8:00 A.M. to 8:00 P.M.
See Chicago listing for details.

Wild Oats Community Market
Wild Oats Plaza
764 Buffalo Grove Road
Buffalo Grove, IL 60089
(847) 419-9080
Hours   Monday through Saturday 7:00 A.M. to 10:00 P.M.; Sunday 7:00 A.M. to 9:00 P.M.
A delightfully designed store with a fun shopping environment, this new-to-the-Chicago-area natural foods chain offers one-stop shopping for people who want to live a healthy lifestyle. They offer everything related to good health, from food that is minimally processed and free of artificial ingredients and preservatives to earth-friendly household products. The meat, seafood, and poultry department and the produce section are mostly organic. There's a nutrition section with an array of supplements plus some essential oils and an impressive health and beauty department. Like many stores, Wild Oats also has a prepared foods department where customers can get freshly made sandwiches, soups, and salad. There's also a sushi bar.

South/Southwest Suburbs

For the Good of It, Limited
3135 W. Jefferson Street
Joliet, IL 60435
(815) 744-7659
Hours   Monday 9:30 A.M. to 7:00 P.M.; Tuesday through Friday 9:30 A.M. to 6:00 P.M.; Saturday 9:30 A.M. to 5:00 P.M.; closed Sunday.
Folks from all around the Joliet area visit this strip-mall spot not only for the wide variety of nutritional products and organic foods it offers, but also for alternative therapy counseling. Owner Kathy Mazur is a licensed nutritionist and sees customers by appointment only. There's also a chiropractor on the premises who is also a Chinese acupuncturist.

Glenbrook Health Foods
120 Halsted Street
Chicago Heights, IL 60411
(708) 755-9440
Hours   Monday through Friday 9:30 A.M. to 6:30 P.M.; Saturday 9:30 A.M. to 5:00 P.M.; closed Sunday.
A small but well-supplied natural food store, Glenbrook Health Foods boasts a wide selection of vitamins, minerals, herbs, and packaged and refrigerated food items. Samples of papaya juice and freshly ground peanut butter are available daily to customers at no charge. This place is also known for its frequent product demonstrations of herbs and other nutritional products.

Heritage Health Foods
4051 W. 183rd Street
Country Club Hills, IL 60478
(708) 957-0595
Hours   Monday through Friday 9:00 A.M. to 7:00 P.M.; Saturday 9:00 A.M. to 5:00 P.M.; Sunday 11:00 A.M. to 4:00 P.M.

The sister store of Bonne Santé in Chicago, this spot offers a variety of vitamins, herbs, and homeopathic remedies. There's also plenty of organic packaged goods, plus refrigerated and frozen food items.

Let's Live Health Store
140 W. Sibley Boulevard
Dolton, IL 60419
(708) 849-8343
Hours   Monday through Friday 10:00 A.M. to 8:00 P.M.; Saturday 10:00 A.M. to 6:00 P.M.; closed Sunday.
The only store in the south suburbs with an organic juice bar, this place stocks a variety of natural weight-loss products as well as vitamins, minerals, herbs, aloe vera products, and detoxification teas, plus a few packaged goods and refrigerated items.

Mid-Oak Health Foods and Environmentals
4718 W. 147th Street
Midlothian, IL 60445
(708) 388-3110
Hours   Monday through Friday 9:30 A.M. to 6:30 P.M.; Saturday 9:30 A.M. to 5:00 P.M.; closed Sunday.
The owner of this store, David Grotto, is a registered dietician who provides nutritional counseling to his customers by appointment only. He also conducts evening classes at the store based on a variety of health topics that he discusses on his weekend radio program. Shoppers will find vitamins, herbs, homeopathic remedies, and allergy-free products as well as a moderate selection of health and beauty care items. Grotto also carries air and water purification devices as well as full-spectrum lighting fixtures and replacement bulbs.

New Vitality Health Foods
9177 W. 151st Street
Orland Park, IL 60462

(708) 403-0120

Hours   Monday, Wednesday, and Friday 10:00 A.M. to 6:00 P.M.; Tuesday and Thursday 10:00 A.M. to 9:00 P.M.; Saturday 10:00 A.M. to 5:00 P.M.; closed Sunday.

This strip-mall spot is the place to shop for gluten-, wheat-, and dairy-free foods. They also carry a wide selection of vitamins, minerals, herbs, homeopathic remedies, and cruelty-free body care items.

Sunrise Farm Market
17650 Torrence Avenue
Lansing, IL 60438
(708) 474-6166

Hours   Monday through Friday 9:00 A.M. to 9:00 P.M.; Saturday 9:00 A.M. to 6:00 P.M.; closed Sunday.

This store is one of the best places to shop for natural food items in the South suburbs. Designed much like a mini-health-food supermarket, this natural food mart carries 100 percent organic produce plus a wide selection of organic packaged, frozen, and refrigerated food items. They also stock plenty of organic meat as well as meat alternative products. Shelves stocked with a broad range of nutritional supplements and a few homeopathic products line the south wall of the store. The store's personal care department contains a wide array of all-natural body care products and cosmetics. A full-time cosmetologist is on staff to help customers with their choice of products. The information center is perhaps the best on this side of town; it consists of articles from various health publications, plus brochures and newsletters on various aspects of holistic health.

Tillie's Health Hut
5559 W. 127th Street
Crestwood, IL 60445
(708) 371-1988

Hours Monday through Saturday 10:00 A.M. to 6:00 P.M.; closed Sunday.

The owner of this store, Tillie Deanne, has been in business for more than twenty years and knows most of her customers by name. But whether the people visiting her shop are friends or strangers, Tillie is happy to personally assist them with their selection of nutritional products. The store also stocks vitamins, minerals, herbs, and amino acids. There's also a nice-size bulk food section consisting of nuts, seeds, flours, and grains.

Western Suburbs

Apple Valley Natural Foods
806 E. Ogden Avenue
Westmont, IL 60559
(630) 789-2270
Hours Monday through Thursday 9:00 A.M. to 8:00 P.M.; Friday 9:00 A.M. to 6:00 P.M.; Sunday 10:00 A.M. to 5:00 P.M.

The vegetarian's health food store, Apple Valley offers its customers supplements and herbs, refrigerated food items, bulk grains and flours, specialty breads, including sprouted, and cruelty-free body care products.

C & I Kuhn Health Foods
806 E. Roosevelt Road
Wheaton, IL 60187
(630) 668-3311
Hours Monday through Saturday 9:00 A.M. to 5:00 P.M.; Tuesday 9:00 A.M. to 6:00 P.M.; closed Sunday.

During the first ten years of this fifty-year-old-plus business, the owner sold clothes and gift items. Five years later, the store started selling health food items. Today, they still sell some clothing, but mostly just 100-percent-cotton men's flannel shirts. They also sell vitamins, minerals, herbs, and wheat-free foods. Set up like an old general store, the merchandise in this place is situated on shelves behind the counter and the health and beauty care items are displayed in beautiful antique display cases.

Fruitful Yield
New York Square
4334 E. Fox Valley Center Drive
Aurora, IL 60506
(630) 585-9200
Hours   Monday through Friday 9:30 A.M. to 8:30 P.M.; Saturday 10:00 A.M. to 6:00 P.M.; Sunday 11:00 A.M. to 5:00 P.M.

Fruitful Yield
Cermak Plaza
7003 W. Cermak Road
Berwyn, IL 60650
(708) 788-9103
Hours   Monday through Friday 9:00 A.M. to 8:00 P.M.; Saturday 9:00 A.M. to 6:00 P.M.; Sunday 11:00 A.M. to 5:00 P.M.

Fruitful Yield
Meadowbrook Shopping Center
2129 W. 63rd Street
Downers Grove, IL 60516
(630) 969-7614
Hours   Monday through Friday 9:30 A.M. to 8:30 P.M.; Saturday 9:30 A.M. to 5:30 P.M.; closed Sunday.

Fruitful Yield
214 North York Road
Elmhurst, IL 60126
(630) 530-1445
Hours   Monday and Thursday 9:00 A.M. to 9:00 P.M.; Tuesday and Friday 9:00 A.M. to 6:00 P.M.; Wednesday and Saturday 9:00 A.M. to 5:00 P.M.; closed Sunday.

Fruitful Yield
Willowood Center
2111 Bloomingdale Road
Glendale Heights, IL 60139
(630) 894-2553
Hours   Monday and Thursday 9:30 A.M. to 8:00 P.M.; Tuesday, Wednesday, and Friday 9:30 A.M. to 6:00 P.M.; Saturday 9:30 A.M. to 5:00 P.M.; closed Sunday.

Fruitful Yield
Village Plaza
727 E. Roosevelt Road
Lombard, IL 60148
(630) 629-9242
Hours   Monday and Thursday 9:00 A.M. to 9:00 P.M.; Tuesday, Wednesday, Friday, and Saturday 9:00 A.M. to 6:00 P.M.; closed Sunday.
See North/Northwest Suburbs listing for details.

Here's Health Stores, Inc.
902 N. Lake Street
Aurora, IL 60506
(630) 897-3490
Hours   Monday through Friday 9:30 A.M. to 8:00 P.M.; Saturday 9:30 A.M. to 5:00 P.M.; Sunday 12:00 P.M. to 5:00 P.M.

Here's Health Stores, Inc.
2753 Maple
Lisle, IL 60532
(630) 420-7357
Hours   Monday through Friday 9:30 A.M. to 8:00 P.M.; Saturday 9:30 A.M. to 5:30 P.M.; Sunday 11:00 A.M. to 5:00 P.M.
See Chicago listing for details.

Lone Star Natural Foods
13 E. Main Street
St. Charles, IL 60174

(630) 584-7650
Hours   Monday, Tuesday, Wednesday, Friday, and Saturday 9:00 A.M. to 6:00 P.M.; Thursday 9:00 A.M. to 7:00 P.M.; Sunday 11:00 A.M. to 4:00 P.M.

This place carries a wide selection of vitamins, minerals, homeopathic remedies, and herbs in a variety of forms, including bulk. In addition to organic packaged goods, there are also cruelty-free body care items, aromatherapy products, essential oils, and pet nutrition.

Natural Herbal Products, Inc.
3207 St. Charles Road
Bellwood, IL 60104
(708) 544-0550
Hours   Monday through Friday 10:00 A.M. to 7:00 P.M.; Saturday 9:00 A.M. to 6:00 P.M.; closed Sunday.

This mini-mall mart offers a selection of supplements comparable to larger health food stores but, unlike the mega-markets, customers are able to ask staff members questions regarding nutritional products in an unhurried, friendly atmosphere. Shoppers will find a complete line of vitamin and mineral supplements, including DHEA, melatonin, ginkgo biloba, and herbs in bulk, liquid, and capsule form. There's also frozen and canned foods as well as soy products that cater to a vegetarian lifestyle.

Soup to Nuts
425 Hamilton Street
Geneva, IL 60134
(630) 232-6646
Hours   Monday through Saturday 8:00 A.M. to 7:00 P.M.; Sunday 11:00 A.M. to 5:00 P.M.

In addition to nutritional supplements, Soup to Nuts carries wheat-, gluten-, corn-, yeast-, sugar-, and dairy-free products. This store is an excellent place for people interested in learning about ways to improve their health: it has an area where customers can sit and read the latest Soup to Nuts newsletter, jot down recipes from cookbooks offered in the book section, or eat fruit pies made by Becky's Bakery, a separate business operating within the store.

Whole Foods Market
7245 W. Lake Street
River Forest, IL 60305
(708) 366-1045
Hours   Monday, Tuesday, Wednesday, Thursday, and Sunday 8:00 A.M. to 9:00 P.M.; Friday and Saturday 8:00 A.M. to 10:00 P.M.

Whole Foods Market
151 Rice Lake Square
Wheaton, IL 60187
(630) 588-1500
Hours   Monday through Sunday 8:00 A.M. to 10:00 P.M.
See Chicago listing for details.

4 Learning and Resource Centers

One of the lessons that life constantly tries to teach us is the lesson of unity—if one person suffers, we all suffer. Conversely, when someone succeeds, a rippling effect takes place and many are blessed.

In this chapter, you'll find learning and personal growth centers that are dedicated to helping people become more aware of themselves and the world around them. Several of these places offer classes that revolve around the unity of humankind. Some places even feature lecturers who talk about people's connection to the earth. Others focus on healing and spirituality.

You won't find any continuing education classes here that are offered by local universities, colleges, or park districts. With the exception of the C. G. Jung Institute, these places won't give you credits toward an academic degree. The instructors won't even reprimand you if you don't complete your homework. The faculty at these centers understand that your participation in class is a part of your personal journey through life and they allow you the freedom to set your own pace.

Unfortunately, there are no full-fledged holistic learning and resource centers in the South/Southwest suburbs; however, the Common Ground Center sometimes offers classes in Tinley Park.

Chicago

Healing Earth Resource Center
2570 N. Lincoln Avenue
Chicago, IL 60614
(773) EAR-THLY
This is the only learning center in the Chicago area where students can shop for books, clothes, and incense after class and then sit down for a delicious vegetarian meal at the center's restaurant, The Mother Earth Café and Organic Juice Bar. Healing Earth Resource Center is one of the premier centers for people interested in holistic health and living. They offer courses in yoga and tai chi. They also conduct classes in creativity, spirituality, and meditation. Students can also make appointments with holistic practitioners who rent space here for body work and energy field work such as Reiki. Class fees vary from free admission to $120 for a six-week session.

The School of Exceptional Living
445 E. Ohio, Suite 260
Chicago, IL 60611
(312) 329-1200
A center with the motto "I do it exceptionally," this place equips students with tools to help themselves live fulfilling lives. They offer personal development and psychological, spiritual, and self-discovery programs that are divided into four areas of concentration: Living Spirit consists of courses that focus on spirituality and conscious living; Living Visions offers classes and seminars that revolve around personal growth and spiritual development; Unity in Action features programs directed at single men and women plus families and couples; and Vision in Action offers workshops and classes for people seeking support in their businesses and careers. In addition to offering various self-development classes, they also sponsor

spiritual retreats on a yearly basis that include trips to sacred places within this country and abroad. There are also two excellent support groups that emphasize holistic healing and living: the Men's Guild and the Women's Circle. All activities in the school have two components: Karma cleansing and gift development. Karma cleansing simply refers to finishing what you've started in every aspect of your life, and gift development is the recognition, acknowledgment, acceptance, and expression of your unique talents. Fees for classes range from $15 per session for a continuous evening course to $475 for local weekend retreats.

Transitions Learning Center
1750 N. Kingsbury
Chicago, IL 60622
(312) 932-9076
The Chicago area's premiere resource for books on alternative health treatments, spirituality, and healing, Transitions Bookplace and Café opened a learning center in the summer of 1998 just around the corner from the bookstore (1000 W. North Avenue). Authors who give free book discussions at the store now offer workshops at the learning center. Fees for these workshops begin at $15. Transitions' book club members receive a reduced rate and a seasonal catalog featuring upcoming presentations. Past workshop titles include Hawaiian Shamanism, Meditation: The Secret Path to the Garden Within, and Feng Shui Your Life. Holistic health providers also offer workshops at the Learning Center. The café offers coffee, tea, and a few vegetarian items such as soups and sandwiches.

North/Northwest Suburbs

C. G. Jung Institute of Chicago
1567 Maple Avenue
Evanston, IL 60201
(847) 475-4848

A place for the soul to rest and refresh, this not-for-profit adult education center offers classes, lectures, and workshops based upon the teachings of Swiss psychiatrist Carl Gustave Jung, a pioneer in the exploration of the human psyche. One of the goals of this institution is to promote programs that tap into the deep reservoir of potential that lies within each individual. One of the ways they do this is by offering a variety of classes based upon Jung's teachings for both the layperson and professional. Classes aimed at the general public are designed to stimulate self-understanding, which is not knowledge of the ego, but an awareness and acceptance of one's own unconscious. The folks at the institute feel that only when an individual loves, understands, and appreciates him- or herself can he or she then make positive changes in the society. For those who aren't interested in taking classes but would like to learn more about Jungian psychology, the bookstore stocks over 2,500 titles in analytical psychology and related topics such as anthropology, mythology, fairy tales, art therapy, spirituality, religion, philosophy, and women's and men's studies. There's also a library that contains books and audio and video tapes on the same subjects. A referral service is offered to people interested in undertaking Jungian analysis. An annual membership program is also available and includes associate memberships for $30, full memberships for $70, and a discounted rate for seniors and full-time students at $50. Fees for classes offered at this school start at $12 per session.

Common Ground Center
815 Rosemary Terrace
Deerfield, IL 60015
(847) 940-7870
Interested in learning more about world religion, history, mysticism, and philosophy? Then take a course at this place where people of various backgrounds and traditions have gathered for more than twenty years to discuss, learn, and study a variety of subjects such as the oneness of mankind and Eastern and Western religion. Some of the core classes offered include: Western Ways to the Center—a study of the classical Western religions such as Judaism, Christianity, Islam, and Zoroastrianism, and Eastern Ways to the Center—an exploration of Hinduism, Buddhism, Jainism, Sikhism, Taoism, and Confucianism. Class fees start at $12 per session. Courses are sometimes offered in Chicago at the River North Building, 920 N. Franklin Street; in the North/Northwest suburbs at Lakeside Center, 401 Country Club Road, Crystal Lake; and in the South/Southwest suburbs at Tinley Park High School, 6111 175th Street, Tinley Park. A variety of annual membership packages are also available.

Infinity Foundation
1282 Old Skokie Road
Highland Park, IL 60035
(847) 831-8828
This not-for-profit, nonsectarian foundation offers some of the best courses on holistic health in the area. Class topics range from Introductin to Meditation and Homeopathic Remedy Kit for the Home to special workshops such as Your Heart's Desire, a seminar that helps you realize your goals. The Infinity Foundation also offers rites of passage, ceremonies, and services through Akeva, their spiritual community. Some of these cer-

emonies include commitment ceremonies for couples who want to honor their connection to one another without the legal sanction of marriage, and memorial remembrances, which are not funerals, but spiritually oriented celebrations to honor someone who has recently died. The center also offers healing circles, spiritual support groups, and meditation classes through Akeva. Class fees average about $25 for an evening seminar and up. The annual membership fee is $50.

Oasis Center
624 Davis Street
Evanston, IL 60201
(847) 475-7303
One of the country's oldest personal-growth centers, this thirty-year-old not-for-profit adult education spot attracts well-known leaders in the area of holistic health and living, spirituality, psychology, and self-awareness. This place frequently features lectures given by some of the country's best-known authors in the field of personal development. Past speakers include Dr. Elisabeth Kubler-Ross, author of *On Death and Dying*; Sam Keen, author of *Fire in the Belly*; and Dr. Deepak Chopra, author of *Quantum Healing*. Annual membership fees range from $35 for a regular membership to $350 for a lifetime membership. The cost of classes and workshops range from $12 for an evening group to about $250 for an intensive two-day workshop.

Western Suburbs

Theosophical Society
1926 N. Main Street
Wheaton, IL 60189
(630) 668-1571
The Theosophical Society is not a religious organization; rather, it is a worldwide, nonsectarian organization that was founded in 1875 by Helena Petrovna Blavatsky and Colonel Henry Steel Olcott. Its American headquarters are located here on a forty-two-acre estate that consists of a mansion, residential housing, and beautiful gardens. The organization's educational arm is called Olcott Institute and offers classes, lectures, seminars, and workshops on the comparative study of religion, philosophy, and science. The Wisdom of the Tao Te Ching, The Universe Is in Us, and Daily Life As Spiritual Practice are examples of past class titles. In addition, they offer weekly tai chi, yoga, and meditation classes plus lectures on various holistic healing therapies. There's also a library and bookstore on the premises. The annual membership fee is $37.50 and class fees begin at $6.

5 Meditation in Motion Classes

This book wouldn't be complete without a chapter devoted to exercise. Here's a list of resources offering programs that will not only keep you physically fit, but will also help you stay emotionally and spiritually centered and teach you forms of movement therapy that are meditative. These programs include activities like dance therapy, yoga, and tai chi.

There are all kinds of dance classes in the Chicago area, but the dance workshops, therapists, and instructors who are listed in this section conduct dance programs that are specifically designed to help you reconnect with your inner being. I've also listed a program that uses dance to help facilitate world peace and spiritual understanding. What I have not listed in this book are ballet, tap, jazz, and other classes that emphasize dance strictly as an art form, or programs that emphasize physical strengthening. Although the resources on the following pages recognize dance as a form of creative expression, they also use dance as a means to heal on an emotional and spiritual level.

You can find many yoga studios in the Chicago metropolitan area where students learn various styles of this five-thousand-year-old Eastern Indian relaxation system from certified yoga instructors. Most studios offer introductory classes for those just beginning yoga. In these classes, initiates learn classical Hatha yoga before they are trained in other styles such as the Iyengar method, which involves the use of props, or Ashtanga Vinyasa yoga, a variation which entails long, flowing movements. There are also intermediate classes for advanced students, and some places, like the Himalayan Institute, offer teacher certification programs.

Yoga studios are located in either rented commercial space or in the homes of certified yoga instructors. Some organizations like the Sivanada Group and the Himalayan Institute own buildings in which they teach yoga as a way of life. The yoga studios located in commercial space usually have less stringent hours and offer more courses throughout the day than those that are situated in a home. Some of these places even include a retail sales area. Studios that are set up in homes typically have very specific hours and are located in a place in the house other than the regular living space, such as a basement. Some students prefer these studios over storefront studios because they find the atmosphere more intimate.

Regardless of where the studio is located, one of the things I like about local yoga centers is that they offer continuous yoga classes, which means if you decide to go on vacation or take a break from class for a while, there will always be another session that you can participate in when you're ready to resume.

Yoga has many therapeutic benefits, including making the body more limber and eliminating stress. Some yogis even see it as a kind of meditation. "It helps keep me centered," says certified yoga instructor Sharon Steffensen, who edits *YogaChicago*, a free resource guide of yoga activities in the Chicago area. "It's more than stretching and handling stress. As you do it, you go deep into places inside yourself where you have stored issues and traumas from childhood. But the deeper you go into your practice, you'll get flashes of insight. All of a sudden you'll think, 'You know, I'm a good person after all despite all the things that have happened in the past.' You're not clouded so much by your emotions and issues," she says.

Although most of the following studios are devoted to yoga, some of them also offer courses in tai chi and different forms of dance. Like yoga, tai chi is another ancient form of exercise that keeps mind, body, and spirit centered.

Tai chi is a noncombative martial art based upon taoist principles. There are various styles of tai chi: Chen, Lee, Yang, and Wu. In class, you'll become acquainted with the form, the basis for any tai chi practice. A form consists of slow-moving, graceful exercises performed in a pattern. The type of form an instructor teaches varies from the long form, which can consist of as many as 108 movements, or the short form, which involves only 37 or 48 movements. One type of tai chi practice called tai chi chih, designed primarily for stress reduction and relaxation, uses only twenty movements.

Like most yoga classes, tai chi sessions also last ninety minutes and usually begin with warm-up exercises. Some instructors incorporate qi gong, which loosely translated means "energy work," throughout the class session to help students become aware of their energy.

"During class I ask my students to think about the relationship between tai chi and their acupuncture meridians," says Alan Uretz, who teaches classes at American WholeHealth, an integrative medicine clinic located in the city. "Then I ask them to think about the energy they feel and how it relates to their health and their connection to the universe," he says.

Tai chi is taught at various places in the Chicago area such as holistic health-care facilities, metaphysical bookstores, park districts, cultural centers, martial arts academies, and even in the heath clubs of some apartment buildings. However, unlike yoga, there are not many places that devote their entire class schedule to tai chi.

I have included the names of some of the best dance, tai chi, and yoga instructors in town. A few of these teachers offer classes in both the city and suburbs.

Regardless of which moving meditation class you choose, however, you may not achieve the flattened stomach or defined abdominal muscles that you can get after working out consistently at a health club, but what you will notice is an emerging inner light, increased energy, and peace of mind.

Locations Vary

Gabrielle Roth's Ecstatic Dance
Karyn Tonkinson
(773) 381-5506 for information on classes, workshops, and gatherings
Karyn Tonkinson is this area's only certified teacher for Gabrielle Roth's Ecstatic Dance practice. During this weekend program, participants are encouraged to dance to the beat of five rhythms that, along with breath work, help them explore memories and release pent-up emotions. Tonkinson describes it as "introspective spiritual movement practice." The Roth 5 Rhythms class is recommended for beginners. Other programs include Waves and Heartbeat. Sweat Your Prayers is a bimonthly event where participants practice the 5 Rhythms in a safe, nonthreatening environment. The fee for Sweat Your Prayers is $10 per session.

Trance Dance
Turning Point Productions
(847) 446-2081
Trance Dance is a type of shamanic dance in which participants begin with an intention to heal some aspect of themselves or a condition in their lives. Once participants' intentions are acknowledged, they celebrate the resolution of

these problems through dance. During this moving meditation, participants are blindfolded as they dance to various kinds of rhythms, ranging from Middle Eastern to Northern African music. The dance helps a participant release the ego, and reacquaint the dancer with his or her spirit. Certified Trance Dance presenter Gregg Austensen conducts monthly Trance Dance workshops throughout Chicago and the surrounding suburbs. The cost for a three-hour session is $15 in advance and $20 at the door. Call Turning Point Productions for an updated schedule.

Chicago

The Body-Mind Connection
4740 N. Lincoln Avenue
Chicago, IL 60625
(773) 728-7175
This second-floor spot offers a self-discovery dance class incorporating free dancing, neuro-linguistic programming, and journaling. Faculty members also teach weekly tai chi and yoga classes. The Kundalini yoga class is an all-time favorite and involves plenty of movement as well as deep breathing. The fee for the six-week dance class is $60. The tai chi and yoga classes cost $7 per session.

Global Yoga and Wellness Center
1823 W. North Avenue
Chicago, IL 60622
(773) 489-1510
This yoga studio, located in the Wicker Park/Bucktown area, is owned and managed by a registered nurse, Rhonda Kantor, R.N., B.S.N. This health-care practitioner and certified yoga instructor teaches beginning Hatha yoga, prenatal yoga, and a yoga class that teaches students postures to eliminate back

pain. Other types of yoga taught at the center include Iyengar yoga and Kundalini yoga as well as special yoga sessions for people with round, tall, and large bodies. Tai chi and belly dance classes, on-site chair massage sessions, and mother/baby wellness and parenting group classes are also held at this site. A four-class package is $35 for most sessions and must be used within a six-week period. The drop-in fee is $10. The belly dancing class is a four-week course and costs $40. The chair-massage rates are $10 for ten minutes; $15 for fifteen minutes; and $20 for twenty minutes.

Narayanananda Universal Yoga Center
3047 N. Lincoln Avenue, Suite 320
Chicago, IL 60657
(773) 327-3650
This yoga studio, directed by Suddha Weixler, is the premier spot for Ashtanga Vinyasa yoga. Located on the North Side, this spot features other yoga classes such as Hatha, Iyengar, and prenatal. The studio, which is located in a space with large windows, wood flooring, and high ceilings, also contains a retail area where students can buy mats, blocks, and straps for their home practice. The drop-in rate is $13 per class.

Northwest Tai Chi Academy
3516 W. Fullerton Avenue
Chicago, IL 60641
(773) 772-1621
One of the few places in the area that teaches the philosophy behind tai chi as well as offers classes, the faculty at this storefront instructs students in the traditional temple-style tai chi. Individuals can sign up for individual instruction, a good choice for beginners, or a beginning advanced class, designed for those with a little more experience. Standing and sitting meditation classes are also available. Classes are $50 a month for unlimited sessions.

The Peace School
3121 N. Lincoln Avenue
Chicago, IL 60657
(773) 248-7959
A twenty-two-year-old not-for-profit organization designated by the United Nations as a peace messenger, this school has some of the most unique moving meditation classes in the Chicago area. Classes were developed by the school's founder, Myung Su Y. S. Kim. This spot offers classes in peace breathing and meditation, a combination of deep breathing and peaceful thinking; peace exercise, a technique that incorporates the peace breathing method along with movement based upon the original system of yoga; and peace exercise plus, a type of exercise that combines the other techniques with acupressure and massage to facilitate the stimulation of internal organs. This place also offers traditional martial art and self-defense classes for men, women, and children. Class fees range from $40 for a four-week class to $70 for an eight-week session.

Sivananda Yoga Vedanta Center
1246 W. Bryn Mawr Avenue
Chicago, IL 60660
(773) 878-7771
One of the oldest yoga centers in Chicago, this place has been offering classes since 1972 and is part of an international group founded by the late Swami Vishnu-Devananda, who is recognized worldwide as a leading authority on Hatha and Raja yoga. They offer beginning and intermediate classical yoga classes, meditation courses, special workshops and events such as vegetarian cooking classes and fasting weekend retreats, plus yoga classes for children. Teacher training courses are held off site. Most courses at this center are five weeks long and last for ninety minutes. Class fees are $50 for a five-week course. The drop-in fee is $8. Membership packages are also available.

Senior citizens and students with an ID get 10 percent off memberships, classes, and workshops.

The Temple of Kriya Yoga
2414 N. Kedzie
Chicago, IL 60647
(773) 342-4600
Best known for its Hatha yoga teacher certification program, the temple offers continuous Hatha yoga classes on Sunday and other classes throughout the week. Faculty members also teach meditation courses in which students learn how, why, and when to meditate. There's also a retail store that stocks books on meditation, yoga, and other spiritual topics. Class fees start at $7 per session.

Yoga Circle
401 W. Ontario
Chicago, IL 60611
(312) 915-0750
Located in downtown Chicago just across the hall from Biosystems, a preventive health-care facility, this comfy place contains two beautiful yoga studios equipped with several yoga props. Instructors at Yoga Circle teach various courses in Iyengar yoga all day ranging from introductory sessions to level 4 and 5 classes for more experienced students and teachers. Restorative yoga classes are also offered around lunchtime to help students relax and take the edge off. Director Gabriel Halpern conducts special yoga workshops throughout the year, such as Back Care Basics. He also organizes other gatherings not related to yoga, such as the men's support group and solstice celebrations. There's a small concession shop inside the studio that stocks various items to assist students with their home practice, such as sticky mats, pranayama pillows, and neti pots. The initial registration fee is $20 for new students. Class fees range from $44 for a series of four classes to $75 for a series of ten classes. The drop-in rate is $13 per class.

North/Northwest Suburbs

Bodyscapes
820 Davis Street, Suite 216
Evanston, IL 60201
(847) 864-6464
This place started out as a massage therapy center ten years ago and has since grown into a therapeutic massage and yoga studio. Longtime yoga students as well as people who just love to dance will enjoy the yoga dance class; no triple turns or pirouettes are required here. This eight-week session combines Middle Eastern, African, jazz, and modern dance with a traditional yoga warm-up. They also offer periodic classes with music provided by a live percussionist. In the yoga therapeutics class, students learn different postures that help alleviate neck and back pain. Beginning yoga classes are also listed on the class schedule. Class fees start at $96 for an eight-week session. Therapeutic massages are available by appointment only.

The Evanston School of Yoga
1122 Seward Street
Evanston, IL 60202
(847) 869-7221
Located in a home where one of the rooms has been designated for yoga, this place offers continuous classes in Hatha yoga and tai chi. They also conduct workshops in Kriya yoga, meditation, and the healing system of Ayurvedic medicine. Class fees average about $10 per session.

The Himalayan Institute's Holistic Health Center
1505 Greenwood Road
Glenview, IL 60025
(847) 724-0300
One of the premier spots for Hatha yoga in the Chicago area, this institute offers Beginning 1, Beginning 2, and Intermedi-

ate yoga classes plus children's yoga and gentle yoga sessions for seniors. It has continuous tai chi, qi gong, and meditation classes, and a course entitled Relaxation and Breathing. Special workshops such as Kundalini and partner yoga are held throughout the year. Hatha yoga teacher training is also available. Hatha yoga class fees are $55 for an eight-week session or $10 per session; the meditation class is a six-week session and costs $65; and the relaxation and breathing class is a four-week course and costs $50. Children's yoga classes are eight weeks in duration and cost $26 for kids ages 3 to 6, and $32 for youth ages 7 to 10. Tai chi classes are $60 for six weeks and qi gong classes are $240 for twelve classes. There's also a Hatha pass that allows unlimited participation for a six-month period in any or all of the Hatha yoga classes for $150. Members and seniors receive discounts on most classes. Satellite classes are offered by Brunette Eason, (773) 660-1239, on the South Side of Chicago.

Lakeside Yoga and Massage Center
949 Ridge Avenue
Evanston, IL 60602
(847) 866-2818
Located in the basement of a home owned by yoga instructor and certified massage therapist Monika Christina Andrea, this peaceful place features yoga classes in the Iyengar method and contains two massage rooms and a hydrotherapy room with a hot tub. There's also a yoga studio with a fireplace and several yoga props such as ropes, mats, swings, pillows, bolsters, and balls. This place offers beginning and advanced classes, plus restorative and prenatal sessions. Andrea also provides yoga classes for kids and gives therapeutic massages. A six-week yoga session is $66; one yoga session is $14; and a children's yoga session is $10 for a forty-five-minute class. A sixty-minute massage starts at $60.

Malter Institute
2500 W. Higgins Road, Suite 355
Hoffman Estates, IL 60159
(847) 519-0220
Certified yoga instructor and psychotherapist Rosalie Malter teaches various styles of yoga at her home studio located in the North/Northwest suburbs. She offers beginning and intermediate Hatha yoga classes and also teaches the Iyengar method. Most classes are eight-week sessions, but students are free to drop in on days when it's convenient. Malter also conducts special workshops at her studio, including yoga for menopause and a yoga and juice fast weekend. An eight-week yoga class is $72. The drop-in fee is $13 per class and workshop fees start at $50.

Shanti Niwas
1305 Merrill Road
Algonquin, IL 60102
(847) 854-2047
Another yoga studio located in a home, the classes offered at this place focus on the meditative aspect of yoga. Course offerings at Shanti Niwas, a Sanskrit word meaning "peaceful abode," include beginning and intermediate classical Hatha yoga, Kundalini yoga, Iyengar yoga, and meditation classes. This place also holds vegetarian cooking courses and sponsors yoga meditation retreats. Most yoga classes are eight weeks in duration and start at $60, with a drop-in fee of $10. The four-week meditation course is $55.

White Iris Yoga
1822 N. Ridge Avenue
Evanston, IL 60201
(847) 864-9987
One of the most beautiful yoga studios in the Chicago area, this place occupies 1,000 square feet and features oak wood

floors, skylights, and a ceiling that's twenty feet high. Owner Paula Kout, the official yoga instructor for the Chicago Bulls, teaches a variety of Hatha yoga classes, including an excellent four-week orientation class for new initiates and weekly beginning and intermediate classes. Kout also offers two special workshops a year: The Restorative Pose and Partner Yoga. The studio also contains a retail center that offers plenty of yoga accessories for sale, including leggings, T-shirts, incense, tapes, and yoga props. Class fees average about $15 for a ninety-minute session.

South/Southwest Suburbs

Earth and Beyond New Age Center
15931 S. Harlem Avenue
Tinley Park, IL 60477
(708) 429-9681
This metaphysical bookstore and retail shop offers Hatha yoga classes on Monday and Thursday evenings taught by Reneé Garrick, a certified Hatha yoga instructor from the Temple of Kriya Yoga. This spot also offers a weekly tai chi class. Hatha yoga classes are $50 for a five-week session. Call for information regarding the latest tai chi class.

Reneé Garrick's Yoga Studio
4306 Applewood Lane
Matteson, IL 60443
(708) 283-0773
This yoga studio is located in the home of Reneé Garrick, a certified yoga instructor. Classes offered at this location include beginning and continuing Hatha yoga sessions. Garrick also offers private yoga classes, yoga consultations, and Phoenix Rising Yoga Therapy. The Hatha yoga class fee is $7.50 for a sixty-minute session. Private yoga lessons start at $25. The yoga consultation and Phoenix Rising Yoga Therapy start at $65.

Western Suburbs

Sanctuary Crystals
5524 Cal-Sag Road
Alsip, IL 60803
(708) 396-2833
This metaphysical bookstore offers a continuous yoga class for all levels on Wednesday evenings taught by certified Hatha yoga instructor MeShall Simmons. In this class, students learn classical Hatha and Kemetic yoga, a style of yoga which is believed to have been practiced in ancient Egypt. Class fees are $10 per session.

Dances of Universal Peace
Shem Center for Interfaith Spirituality
316 Lake Street
Oak Park, IL 60302
(708) 788-2460
The director of the Shem Center for Interfaith Spirituality, Brother Joseph Kilikevice, is the area's main organizer and instructor of the Dances of Universal Peace, a sacred group dance which was created by Samuel Lewis, a resident of the San Francisco Bay area, in the 1960s. This moving meditation involves people joining hands in a circle and dancing as they engage in rituals such as singing and chanting taken from several religious traditions including Christianity, Buddhism, Sufism, Hinduism, and Native North American cultures. This dance is designed to facilitate world peace and to help promote religious understanding. Special programs are also offered around the city. Call for a current schedule.

Garden of Yoga
6B S. LaGrange Road
LaGrange, IL 60525
(708) 802-1329

Located in the Impact Dance studio, this place offers Hatha and Iyengar yoga classes; yoga props are available on the premises. There are also special yoga workshops held on the third Sunday of every month to help students continue their practice. A regular yoga course lasts ninety minutes and is $10 per class. The intermediate class lasts 120 minutes and is $12 per class.

Glass Court Swim & Fitness Center
830 E. Roosevelt Road
Lombard, IL 60148
(630) 629-3390
This is a great place for beginning students to learn classical Hatha yoga. Classes at this health club are held for an eight-week period and cost $30. Ambitious students may want to buy an aerobic punch pass, which gets them more class sessions for their money. Packages include sixteen classes within an eight-week period (two classes per week) for $40, and twenty-four classes within an eight-week period (three classes per week) for $50.

Gottlieb Fitness Center
551 W. North Avenue
Melrose Park, IL 60160
(708) 450-5790
The place to go for a yoga class or two, especially if you're on a tight budget, this health and fitness center offers continuous Hatha yoga classes two times a week in the morning and evening. Class fees are free for members of the health club and just $5 for nonmembers. This spot also offers tai chi and water tai chi classes.

Naper Olympic Health Club
101 E. 75th Street
Naperville, IL 60540
(630) 357-7200

Hatha yoga classes are taught five times a week at this health club by certified instructors from the Himalayan Institute. Class fees are $10 per class or buy a punch card and take ten classes within a three-month period for $80. There's a total membership club package that includes the use of health club facilities plus free yoga classes. Classes last sixty minutes and are suitable for all ages and levels.

Dance, Tai Chi, and Yoga Instructors of Note

The following is a list of dance, tai chi, and yoga instructors who will help you investigate or further explore this form of movement. Some are affiliated with local movement centers and some are independent.

Dance Instructors

Gina Demos
Chicago
(312) 461-9826

Kris Larsen
Chicago
(312) 405-9475

Lara Polski
Chicago
(773) 528-1099

Tai Chi Instructors

Walter Beckley
Chicago and South/Southwest suburbs
(708) 481-9128

Helen Chen
Chicago
(773) 752-2824

Master Yu Cheng Huang
North/Northwest suburbs
(847) 679-3113

Daniel Pesina
Chicago
(773) 296-8410

Reneé Ryan
Western suburbs
(630) 260-1084

Alan Uretz
Chicago
(773) 296-6700

Mfundishi Olafemi A. Watangulizi
Chicago and South/Southwest suburbs
(773) 374-5266

Paula Weiner
Chicago
(773) 883-4944

Yoga Instructors
Joan Budilovsky
Western suburbs
(630) 963-1906

Kay Clay
Western suburbs
(630) 963-4252

Rosalia Holt
Chicago, South/Southwest, and Western suburbs
(773) 488-3820

Yiser Ra Hotep (Elvrid Lawrence)
Chicago
(773) 924-0474

William Hunt
Chicago and Western suburbs
(708) 445-0392

Michael LaRocca
South/Southwest suburbs
(708) 388-3397

Judy Lipke
Western suburbs
(630) 620-1444

Becky Love
Chicago
(312) 225-8871

Patti Slama
Chicago
(708) 386-9848

Susan Witz
Chicago and all suburbs
(312) 944-0855

6 Relaxation Places

When I worked as an advertising account executive, I rarely took time to relax. Back then, my major goal in life was to make a lot of money so that I could build my dream house on the hill and travel to Asia, Africa, and Europe once I retired. Ironically, the only way I knew how to make this happen was by working myself to death. I knew all too well that the long hours I was putting in at work coupled with only four hours of sleep would ultimately affect my health, but I didn't care. What mattered was that I was young, energetic, and on a fast career track. But after five years of racing up the rungs of the corporate ladder, my body began to slow down. Before I knew it, I was twenty pounds overweight and stressed. I lost the stamina it took to climb the ladder of success and, by the time I turned thirty, I stumbled out of the race. I quit my job with no plans of working right away and for six-and-a-half months did nothing but rest. Don't wait until you burn out like I did to take care of yourself!

"If you take time out to relax, it helps you — as you go about your duties and tasks in everyday life — become more functional, more productive, and happier," says Michele Madison, coordinator of Mercy Hospital and Medical Center's Wellspace and Less Stress Program, an educational division that's dedicated to teaching patients different techniques for alleviating stress.

In doing research for this chapter, I talked with several people who have very demanding schedules, but take mini-retreats when they find they're about to be—or already are—overwhelmed. What are mini-retreats? A day, weekend, or afternoon when you forget about work and the responsibilities of home and escape to a private place for some rest, relaxation, and a bit of pampering. The good news is that you don't have to travel far or spend a lot of money on a vacation to get a little R and R.

The resources listed in this chapter are hedonistic haunts located close to Chicago. A few of the places I've included are day spas. They're called day spas because you can literally spend an entire day at one of these places getting your hair styled and nails manicured plus get a body wrap, massage, facial, and pedicure. "Our services are designed to make you feel good all over—from the top of your head all the way down to your toes," says Carolyn Christensen, general manager of the Elizabeth Arden Red Door Salon and Spa, one of the newest and largest spas in the area.

Whereas day spas promote relaxation and beauty, massage centers tout relaxation and health. The Swedish massage is one of the most requested treatments at these relaxation spots, but other types of body work are usually offered, such as deep tissue, pregnancy, and craniosacral therapy. In addition to massage services, some of these holistic haunts offer Reiki and acupuncture sessions.

Two massage centers I've listed even have certified yoga instructors on staff who give private yoga classes. You can usually get spa services such as herbal and aromatherapy body wraps at these massage centers. For those of you who enjoy the therapeutic benefits of water, I've listed a place where you can vegetate in a deprivation tank—a tub filled with salt water that has been known since the early 1960s to have a calming effect on the mind as well as the body. I've also listed establishments with relaxation equipment familiar to most people:

hot and cold tubs and saunas. If you long to get away from familiar scenery, I've included a destination spa located in a bucolic setting just eighty miles south of Chicago.

There are even some massage facilities located in full-service hair salons and health clubs. Although there are some very good ones in the area, like A Matter of Style, a full-service hair salon that offers spa services in Oak Park, and Spa de LaCour, located in the Bannockburn Club, I have not listed them in this chapter. The resources that I have included consist of stand-alone businesses that are strictly devoted to providing an environment and services that facilitate deep relaxation. When you visit any one of the places mentioned in this section, you can rest assured that wherever you go, staff members will be happy to assist you head to foot.

Chicago

Bettye O. Day Spa
5200 S. Harper Avenue
Chicago, IL 60615
(773) 752-3600
Hours   Tuesday through Friday 10:30 A.M. to 6:30 P.M.; Saturday 10:30 A.M. to 3:30 P.M.; closed Sunday and Monday.
The place to go for affordable spa services, this Hyde Park spot was voted by Vogue magazine in 1993 as the best multi-cultural day spa. This twenty-year-old pampering place offers facials, massages, body polishes, manicures, and pedicures. Designed much like the French spas in Europe, this spa also has a hydrotherapy tub. Facials start at $50; massage treatments start at $50; body polishes and hydrotherapy tub prices start at $115; manicures start at $12; and pedicures start at $35. American Express, Visa, MasterCard, personal checks, and cash are all accepted. Gift certificates are also available.

Elizabeth Arden Red Door Salon and Spa
919 N. Michigan Avenue, Fourth Floor
Chicago, IL 60611
(312) 988-9191
Hours   Monday, Tuesday, Friday, and Saturday 9:00 A.M. to 6:00 P.M.; Wednesday 9:00 A.M. to 7:00 P.M.; Thursday 9:00 A.M. to 8:00 P.M.; Sunday 10:00 A.M. to 6:00 P.M.
This glamorous getaway occupies an entire floor in what used to be the Playboy building. Their most popular pampering package, the Arden Spa Day, consists of six to eight hours worth of services designed to soothe customers from the tops of their heads to the tips of their toes. It includes a steam shower, salt glow body polish, massage, facial, pedicure, manicure, haircut, and makeover. Clients are also served a low-cal lunch in the salon's cafe. The entrance to this posh place is located on Walton Street right next to the Knickerbocker Hotel. After a quick elevator ride to the fourth floor, look for the Elizabeth Arden bright red door. The price for the Arden Spa Day is $275. American Express, Visa, MasterCard, personal checks, traveler's checks, and cash are all accepted. Gift certificates are also available.

Mario Tricoci
277 E. Ontario Street
Chicago, IL 60611
(312) 915-0960
Hours   Monday through Thursday 9:00 A.M. to 9:00 P.M.; Friday 9:00 A.M. to 8:00 P.M.; Saturday 9:00 A.M. to 5:00 P.M.; Sunday 10:00 A.M. to 5:00 P.M.
The largest day spa chain in the area, Tricoci has a total of nine spas located in the city and suburbs. They provide a wide variety of pampering services, including nine different types of facial treatments, hair styling services, manicures, pedicures, body wraps, massages (Swedish, peppermint oil, and duo massage treatments are a few customer favorites), and face, leg,

and bikini waxes. The massage therapists on staff at the Oak Brook, Naperville, and Old Orchard spas offer Reiki sessions. Although each spa is decorated in its own unique way, most facilities are equipped with a vanity area, lockers, and Vichy shower with a wet room and hydrotherapy tub. Facials range from $50 to $105. Body treatments range from $35 to $105 while massage and Reiki treatments start at $60. Haircuts start at $30. Manicures and pedicures range from $15 to $45. Visa, MasterCard, personal checks, and cash are all accepted. Gift certificates are also available.

See Appendix B for addresses of the other eight Mario Tricoci locations in the Chicago metropolitan area.

Michael Anthony Salon & Day Spa
1001 W. North Avenue
Chicago, IL 60622
(312) 649-0707

Hours   Tuesday through Thursday 8:00 A.M. to 9:00 P.M.; Friday 8:00 A.M. to 7:00 P.M.; Saturday 8:00 A.M. to 5:00 P.M.; Sunday 10:00 A.M. to 5:00 P.M.; closed Monday.

The practitioners at this spa use products that are manufactured by Aveda. They offer skin care treatments, haircut and style services, nail services, and body treatments. One of their more popular spa packages is called the Ultimate Day of Beauty and includes a manicure, pedicure, ten-step aromatherapy facial, body polish, stress relieving herbal wrap, massage, blow dry, and a makeup application. This seven-hour package also includes a midday snack and a spa garden lunch. Limousine service is optional. Massage treatments are also available and include Swedish, deep muscle therapy, Shiatsu, sports, and a revitalized aromatic massage for expectant mothers. The Ultimate Day of Beauty is $295; facials start at $65; haircut and style services start at $40; nail services start at $16; body treatments range from $40 to $105; massage services start at $65 for a sixty-minute massage and $100 for a ninety-minute session. American Express, Visa, MasterCard, personal checks, and cash are accepted. Gift certificates are also available.

Paradise Health Spa
2910 W. Montrose Avenue
Chicago, IL 60618
(773) 588-3304
Hours   Open seven days a week 7:00 A.M. to 10:00 P.M.
This spot is divided into male and female quarters and contains whirlpools, hot and cold tubs, plus dry and steam saunas. There's also a relaxation room with a television. Massage treatments and body scrubs are available by appointment only. The entrance fee is $12 plus $2 for a key deposit. Massage treatments start at $40 for sixty minutes. American Express, Visa, MasterCard, and cash are accepted.

Space Time Tanks Flotation Center
2526 N. Lincoln Avenue
Chicago, IL 60614
(773) 472-2700
Hours   Monday through Thursday 12:00 P.M. to 10:30 P.M.; Friday, Saturday, and Sunday 10:30 A.M. to 10:30 P.M.
A city getaway with four sensory deprivation tanks, this place also has mind machines—a contraption comprised of goggles and headphones that use light and sound to help the body attain a relaxed state. There's a licensed massage therapist on staff who gives Swedish massages by appointment only. The fee for a sixty-minute float session is $30. The mind machine rate is $5 per each ten-minute interval and Swedish massage sessions start at $60 for a sixty-minute session. American Express, Visa, MasterCard, personal checks, and cash are accepted.

Thousand Waves Spa
1212 W. Belmont Avenue
Chicago, IL 60657
(773) 549-0700

Hours   Tuesday through Friday 1:00 P.M. to 9:00 P.M.; Saturday and Sunday 11:00 A.M. to 7:00 P.M.; closed Monday.

When you visit this women-only spa, you don't have to bring anything with you but your tired body. When customers walk in off the street, they are immediately greeted by staff members and are given a kimono, towel, washcloth, and lock for their locker. That's all that's really needed at this North Side spot, which was voted by *Chicago* magazine in December 1997 as the best low-priced women's health spa. Designed especially for women, this Japanese-inspired health spa contains a sauna, steam bath, Jacuzzi hot tub, relaxation room, and dressing room with lockers. Their spa baths are my favorite and include a Eucalyptus Steam Bath, which is good for the lungs and bronchial system. Customers are allowed unlimited time in the baths. There's also a relaxation room with chaise lounges plus a short story and poetry library. Massage therapy is offered by appointment only. No toiletries? Don't worry—this place also provides shampoo, lotions, and hair dryers. A spa visit is $15; spa visit with fifteen-minute seated tune-up massage, $30; thirty-minute massage is $40; sixty-minute massage is $50; and an herbal wrap (thirty minutes) is $40. Every massage includes a spa visit. Visa, MasterCard, personal checks, and cash are all accepted. Gift certificates are also available.

Urban Oasis
12 W. Maple Street, Third Floor
Chicago, IL 60610
(312) 587-3500
Hours   Monday 3:00 P.M. to 8:00 P.M.; Tuesday through Thursday 10:00 A.M. to 8:00 P.M.; Friday 9:00 A.M. to 7:00 P.M.; Saturday 9:00 A.M. to 5:00 P.M.; and Sunday 12:00 P.M. to 5:00 P.M.

Another popular place for relieving stress, this spot offers rejuvenating massage sessions and spa treatments in an ideal environment for rest and relaxation. It has three private changing rooms where clients abandon their attire in exchange for kimonos and sandals, and three different kinds of showers:

steam, European, and rain. The types of massage treatment offered includes Swedish, deep tissue, sports, Shiatsu, Thai, neuro-muscular, pregnancy, reflexology, craniosacral therapy, and manual lymphatic drainage. They also provide herbal, aromatherapy, mineral-mud, and seaweed body wraps. Private instruction in yoga and infant massage is also available. A thirty-minute massage starts at $40. Spa treatments range from $35 to $60. American Express, Visa, MasterCard, Discover, personal checks, and cash are all accepted. Gift certificates are also available.

North/Northwest Suburbs

Body Mind Dynamics: Therapeutic Massage and Healing Resources
247 Peterson Road
Libertyville, IL 60048
(847) 549-7110
Hours   Monday through Friday 12:00 P.M. to 8:00 P.M.; Saturday 9:00 A.M. to 6:00 P.M.; closed Sunday.
One of the premiere spots for deep tissue body work, this five-year-old massage and resource center has ten certified massage therapists on staff who practice a range of therapies including Swedish, sports, neuro-muscular, trigger point, and therapeutic massage as well as reflexology, myofascial release, and manual lymphatic drainage. There are also relaxation-enhancing products available for sale, such as bath salts, aromatherapy oils, self-treating Thera Canes, meditative music, and imagery tapes. Prices range from $25 for a thirty-minute massage to $75 for a ninety-minute session. Visa, MasterCard, personal checks, and cash are all accepted. Gift certificates are also available.

Caring Hands Massage Center
896 Greenbay Road
Winnetka, IL 60093
(847) 446-2273
Hours   Monday through Friday 9:30 A.M. to 8:00 P.M.; Saturday and Sunday 9:30 A.M. to 6:00 P.M.
The owner of this thirteen-year-old massage center says that the first thing that people say when they walk in the doors of this place is, "Ahhhhhhhh." This spot is immaculately designed with the clieFnt's good health in mind. The interior features wicker furniture accented with cushions and pillows in various pastel shades and arranged according to the rules of feng shui. An air purification system runs continuously to ensure that the customers who come here breathe fresh air. They also use an ozone and ion generator. But people don't just come here for the clean air and comfortable environment. They primarily come to receive body work of all kinds, including Swedish, Shiatsu, deep tissue, reflexology, and acupressure. Staff members also perform Reiki, both Shen and Mari-El, and zero balancing. Visa, MasterCard, personal checks, and cash are all accepted. Massage and Reiki sessions start at $60 for a sixty-minute session. Gift certificates are also available.

Hands On Therapy
1755 Glenview Road
Glenview, IL 60025
(847) 832-1755
Hours   Monday through Friday 8:30 A.M. to 7:00 P.M.; Saturday 8:30 A.M. to 4:00 P.M.; Sunday 12:00 P.M. to 4:00 P.M.
Named the best of the Midwest by *Allure* magazine, this place has three treatment rooms and eleven massage therapists on staff who give a variety of treatments including Swedish, neuro-muscular, myofascial release, and craniosacral therapy. The owner, Wini Nimrod, says the Oriental-style decor in this

haven makes clients feel as if they're taking a retreat in Japan. A thirty-minute massage starts at $35. Personal checks and cash are accepted. Gift certificates are also available.

Ohashiatsu Chicago
825 Chicago Avenue
Evanston, IL 60202
(847) 864-1130
Hours   (Reception desk) Tuesday through Friday 9:30 A.M. to 2:00 P.M.; appointments available 8:00 A.M. to 8:00 P.M. seven days a week.

This is one of the best places for relaxing a tense body in the Chicago area. The practitioners at this healing center practice a form of body work called Ohashiatsu, which is similar to shiatsu except this therapy incorporates physical manipulation with exercise and meditation. During a session, the client, dressed in loose comfortable clothes, lies on a padded floor while the practitioner moves about, stretching and moving limbs while applying firm but gentle pressure to move and balance energy. Continuous sessions help the client become more familiar with his or her body, reduce stress, and enhance good health. Sessions last approximately fifty to sixty minutes. The first visit with a certified Ohashiatsu instructor is $85. Fees for subsequent visits are $80 per session. Payment may be made with Visa, MasterCard, personal checks, or cash.

South/Southwest Suburbs

Soma Spa
Flossmoor Commons Shopping Center
3329 Vollmer Road
Flossmoor, IL 60422
(708) 957-4400
Hours   Monday 3:00 P.M. to 7:00 P.M.; Tuesday through Thursday 9:00 A.M. to 8:00 P.M.; Friday 9:00 A.M. to 6:00 P.M.; Saturday 9:00 A.M. to 5:00 P.M.; closed Sunday.

Another spa with reasonably priced services, Soma—the Greek word for "living body"—offers massage therapy, body treatments, and facials. The practitioners at this strip-mall spot use Jurlique products, which, according to owner Donna Slimski, are the purest of all spa-type products since they're plant-based. They even carry all-natural makeup that is applied during a makeover or can be purchased along with other relaxation items in this spa's retail center. Body treatments include the seaweed body envelopment, Moor mud treatment, body glow treatment, and soothing leg treatment. Spa packages include A Goddess's Morning, a 150-minute package especially for women that includes a sixty-minute aromatherapy massage, a facial, and makeup application. Men enjoy the Zeus's Slumber, a sixty-minute package that consists of an herbal foot bath plus scalp and foot massage. Individual massage treatments include Swedish, sports, Thai yoga, Shiatsu, on-site seated massage, and Jin Shin Do acupressure facials. A Goddess's Morning is $145 and Zeus's Slumber is $60; facials start at $50; body treatments range from $30 to $65; massage treatments start at $35 for a thirty-minute session, $55 for a sixty-minute session, $75 for a ninety-minute session, and $95 for a 120-minute session. Visa, MasterCard, personal checks, and cash are all accepted. Gift certificates are also available.

Western Suburbs

Almora's Hands of Care
807 W. Garfield Boulevard, First Floor
Oak Park, IL 60304
(708) 383-6659
Hours   (By appointment only.) Monday through Saturday 8:00 A.M. to 10:00 P.M.; closed Sunday.
A small but comfortable spot with a quiet, laid-back setting, this place offers a blend of holistic health services such as therapeutic massage treatments, energy field work, and reflexology, plus pampering services including body wraps, hand and foot treatments, and body masks. The herbal linen body wrap is a customer favorite and facilitates deep relaxation. The owner and sole operator of this place, Almora, is a certified massage therapist and holistic practitioner. She also offers a weight-loss and smoking cessation program that involves hypnotherapy. Body wraps range from $45 to $125; body scrubs are $45 to $55; body masks—clay, seaweed, or mud—range from $45 to $65; hand and foot pampering—facials for hands and feet—are $25 to $35; a sixty-minute massage is $55 and a ninety-minute massage is $85. American Express, Visa, MasterCard, Discover, personal checks, and cash are all accepted. Gift certificates are also available.

Day Escape: The Ultimate Spa
150 E. Ogden Avenue, Second Floor
Westmont, IL 60559
(630) 455-0660
Hours   Monday, Tuesday, Wednesday, and Friday 10:00 A.M. to 7:00 P.M.; Thursday 10:00 A.M. to 9:00 P.M.; Saturday 9:00 A.M. to 4:00 P.M.; closed Sunday.
This holistic haven is owned and operated by Diane Krueger, a licensed aesthetician and body worker, who has designed a wellness and relaxation spot for men and women based on the

philosophy of Chinese medicine. The professionals at Day Escape use a line of products called Phytobiodermie. Krueger says that these products correlate to the Chinese philosophy of the law of the five elements: Earth is represented by the color yellow, Fire is red, Metal is white, Water is black, and Wood is green. The five-element facial is a customer favorite and includes a detoxifying colored clay that corresponds with these elements. There's also the Violet Detoxification Mask that includes an application of yellow clay (representing the spleen) and topped with a layer of violet clay (the shade of the chakra located at the crown of the head). Massage treatments are given by candlelight. Yoga classes and nutritional counseling are also available. Body treatments range from $25 to $175; manicures range from $15 to $20; pedicures range from $30 to $35. A thirty-minute massage is $35 and a sixty-minute massage is $60. Ask about special spa packages—my favorite package includes limousine service to the spa where the driver serves you a glass of freshly squeezed orange juice during your ride. Visa, MasterCard, personal checks, and cash are all accepted. Gift certificates are also available.

Nature's Path: Wellness and Massage Spa
49 1/2 S. Washington Boulevard
Hinsdale, IL 60521
(630) 887-1778
Hours   Tuesday and Thursday 10:00 A.M. to 10:00 P.M.; Wednesday 10:00 A.M. to 8:00 P.M.; Friday and Saturday 10:00 A.M. to 5:00 P.M.; closed Sunday and Monday.
This downtown Hinsdale spot contains five treatment rooms, three private changing rooms with European showers, and a comfy waiting room where clients sip herbal tea, juice, or water while they wait. Aveda's all-natural products are used at this suburban haven that offers a range of massage therapy treatments and services that are typically performed at salons or day spas. Some of the services include full body, prenatal,

aromatherapy, and scalp massages; exfoliation and detoxification treatments, body wraps, foot scrubs, and facials. They also offer yoga, women's self-defense, and stress management classes as well as private nutritional counseling. Prices range from $65 for a sixty-minute massage to $90 for a ninety-minute session. Visa, MasterCard, personal checks, and cash are all accepted.

Pheasant Run Resort & Convention Center
4051 E. Main Street
St. Charles, IL 60174
(800) 999-3319
(630) 584-6300
Hours   (Reservations necessary) Monday through Friday 8:30 A.M. to 7:00 P.M.; Saturday and Sunday 9:00 A.M. to 3:00 P.M. If you don't want to travel to another state for rest and relaxation, but you want a resort atmosphere, Pheasant Run offers a relaxation package that includes several of the accoutrements you'd find at other resort and spa places but for less money. The relaxation package at this resort and convention center, called Fitness Plus Overnight, includes overnight accommodations at the hotel, access to the indoor and outdoor swimming pools, a thirty-minute massage the day of arrival followed by an herbal wrap, and a loofah scrub and facial on the day of departure. You'll also get a spa gift basket that includes an array of body care products that will make you and your partner feel good all over. The rate for this package is $275 per couple (double occupancy). Add a second night for just $83.

Destination Spas

Abbey Resort and Fontana Spa
1 Fontana Boulevard
P.O. Box 50
Fontana, WI 53125
(800) SPA-1000
(414) 275-6811

A ninety-minute drive from Chicago, the Abbey Resort has an indoor and outdoor pool, health club, outdoor tennis courts, outdoor basketball court, three restaurants, two lounges, and a spa that offers more than thirty-three different services. This Wisconsin haunt offers a one-night package called the Spa Spree, which includes access to the Fontana spa facilities where guests are treated to one herbal wrap, one massage, and one facial. They also get to participate in physical fitness classes for two days and have lunch by the spa pool. Rates are $223 per person (double occupancy) from October through April and $237 per person (double occupancy) May through September.

Another getaway package, called the Spa Sampler, is a two-night, three-day stay at the hotel. It includes six gourmet spa meals, one herbal wrap, one hand treatment, one loofah scrub or body polish, one private whirlpool, one body massage, one Scotch hose Swiss shower, one skin analysis and facial, and daily fitness classes. Rates from October 1 through April 30 per person are $566 midweek and $588 for the weekend. Rates from May 1 through September 30 per person are $645 midweek and $700 for the weekend.

The Heartland Spa

1237 E. 600 North Road
Gilman, IL 60938
(815) 683-2182
Reservations: (800) 545-HTLD
Hours   (Administrative Offices) Monday through Friday 9:00 A.M. to 5:00 P.M.

Voted by *Town & Country* magazine as one of the best spas in the Western world, this rural respite occupies a thirty-two-acre estate overlooking a secluded lake and is surrounded by a lush forest and tranquil farmland. There's no need to bring a lot of luggage to this health and fitness spot located just eighty miles south of Chicago. Staff members here provide guests (no more than twenty-eight guests are allowed on the premises at one time) clean sweatsuits on a daily basis throughout their two-, five-, or seven-day stay. The spa area, a converted barn, contains the latest exercise equipment, steam rooms, hot tubs, a sauna, an indoor swimming pool, and rooms in which therapists give massages. The spa also has two lighted outdoor tennis courts. Holistic activities are offered round the clock and include such happenings as aerobic and dance classes, meditation, health lectures, and an hour or two of pampering. Other offerings include nature walks, tai chi, yoga classes, as well as more adventurous activities like the low and high ropes course. Spa services include facials, body scrubs and wraps, and massages. A licensed nutritionist also offers nutritional counseling. Low-fat meals are served daily. The standard room rate is $378 per night for weekdays and $420 per night for weekends. Buy the room at this rate and a friend stays for free.

Indian Oak Resort and Spa
558 Indian Boundary Road
Chesterton, IN 46304
(800) 552-4232
(219) 926-2200
Located two hours from Chicago, this holistic hideaway offers one- and two-night spa retreat packages that include massage treatments, facials, pedicures, manicures, and access to their state-of-the-art health club, complete with universal weight machines, sauna, and steam rooms. These packages also include dinner vouchers. There are hiking and biking trails that twist around the resort and a serene body of water, Lake Chubb, where you can go boating. There are also plenty of shops around the hotel, including an art gallery plus a clothing and antique store. This resort also brings holistic health and living speakers to the hotel. Past lecturers include Wayne Dyer and John Douillard, M.D., an Ayurvedic physician who worked with Deepak Chopra. They also hold a relaxation festival that occurs the first weekend in February. The cost of the one-night Spa Taster, double occupancy in a standard room with a lake view, is $370 per couple on weekdays and $398 per couple on the weekend. The two-night spa package, double occupancy in a standard room with a lake view, is $648 per couple on weekdays and $703 per couple on weekends. These prices are good from March 1 until June 30. Prices increase during the high season, July 1 through October 31, and decrease during the low season, November 1 through February 28. Call for the latest package rates and additional information.

7 Earth-Friendly Stores

At one of the poublic school district offices in the south suburbs, a quilt made of construction paper created by the second-grade students at Arcadia Elementary School in Matteson hangs on the wall near the entrance of the building. This work of art consists of patches that were designed by children ranging in age from seven to nine. The children were asked to create art that depicts something for which they are grateful. Some students drew pictures of their family members, their homes, and their parents' cars, but there were a couple of students who drew illustrations of the earth and even the universe.

As adults, we often take the earth for granted. But it seems that once we take personal responsibility for our health, our concern spills over into other areas of our lives. When we start to understand that the quality of food we eat affects the health of our body, quite naturally, we begin to notice how other products we consume affect our well-being. Some of us go a step further and begin purchasing products that are kind to the environment. Many of us start recycling. Others start buying cosmetics that have not been tested on animals.

The resources listed in this chapter feature retail stores that offer products that are environmentally safe and have not been tested on animals. Some stores even accept empty containers for recycling. You'll also find shops that carry organic coffee, apparel made of natural fiber such as cotton and hemp, toys made of natural material, and natural art supplies. I've also included a few services that reflect a sensitivity toward the preservation of the environment.

I have not included businesses that follow strict environmental guidelines but whose product lines aren't necessarily healthy. One such company is Ben & Jerry's, the famous ice cream company. Although this company is at the top of the list with regards to their dedication to saving the earth, a dose of their ice cream on a regular basis will not improve your health. Since this book is essentially about living a healthier lifestyle, I have omitted them from this chapter. What you will find are businesses that offer products designed to enhance your well-being and, at the same time, help you become a more conscious shopper.

Major Chain Stores

Bath & Body Works
(800) 395-1001 or refer to Appendix B
This chain with twenty-seven stores in the Chicago area carries plenty of no-animal-testing personal care products such as lotions, splash colognes, hair products, and skin care items, several of which are made of natural ingredients including essential oils and vitamins. They also sell an array of accessories for the bath and shower like bath pillows, massage tools, and body sponges. Customers get ten cents for every empty Bath & Body Works bottle they bring in to recycle. This store also has a generous return policy.

The Body Shop
(800) 263-9746 or refer to Appendix B
One of the first international store chains in the area to offer environmentally conscious products, this United Kingdom–

based company offers no-animal-testing bath and personal care products, some of which are made with all-natural ingredients. They sell perfume as well as aromatherapy oils that can be mixed in the customer's favorite bath product or massage oil. Their body butter, designed for normal to dry, dry, and extremely dry skin types, is a best-seller and comes in avocado, nut butter, and mango scents. This place also offers personal care products for infants. Customers receive a twenty-five-cent discount on certain products when they return and refill their bottles. Customers are offered five cents per bottle that they bring in to recycle. There are also flyers in the store to remind customers of their responsibility to the earth and encourage them to get involved in helping preserve the environment.

Crabtree & Evelyn
(800) 272-2873 or refer to Appendix B
Pronounced Crabtree and EVE-lyn, this is yet another chain of stores that got its start in the United Kingdom. This bed and bath shop carries an array of no-animal-testing products including baby care items, personal care goods, and men's and women's fragrances. They also stock a small selection of nightwear such as bathrobes and slippers.

Garden Botanika
(800) 968-7842 or refer to Appendix B
This place offers a slew of personal care items that have not been tested on animals, including lotions, shower gels, soaps, cosmetics, hair products, and a complete line of skin care. They also carry custom-blended fragrances. Customers get five cents off their next purchase for every empty Garden Botanika container they bring in to recycle.

Chicago

Aveda Environmental Lifestyle Store
John Hancock Building
875 N. Michigan Ave.
Chicago, IL 60611
(800) 664-0417
Hours   Monday through Saturday 10:00 A.M. to 7:00 P.M.; Sunday 12:00 P.M. to 6:00 P.M.
The place to go for aromatherapy and plant-based products, this chain has no-animal-testing personal care products, earth-friendly supplies for the home, plus their own line of nutritional supplements. Some of their personal care products include plant-based shampoos, conditioners, and color treatments. They also have an extensive makeup line consisting of mineral oil-free eyeshadows, cedar eye pencils, and cosmetic compact cases made from recycled aluminum. Their chakra fragrance line is based upon the Ayurvedic belief in the seven energy centers. Each of the seven aromas corresponds with one of the chakras. All fragrances sold here are unisex. These stores also offer in-store chair massage sessions at $15 for fifteen minutes, and $30 for thirty minutes. The Northbrook store has a licensed massage therapist on staff who gives full body massages. A thirty-minute session starts at $30.

There are also a few Aveda concept businesses in the Chicago area that include day spas and hair salons where the stylists and/or aestheticians use only Aveda products. Call (800) 328-0849 to find an Aveda concept spa or salon.

Earth Cycle
Century Mall
2828 N. Clark Street, First Floor
Chicago, IL 60657
(773) 665-9900
Hours   Monday through Friday 10:30 A.M. to 9:00 P.M.; Sat-

urday 10:30 A.M. to 6:00 P.M.; Sunday 12:00 P.M. to 6:00 P.M. Located in two kiosks on the ground level of the Century Mall, this place stocks organic clothing, including undergarments and socks made from 100 percent cotton. They also have accessories like purses and wallets constructed from recycled material, plus belts decorated with bottle caps and buckles borrowed from recycled seatbelts. Other items include no-animal-testing personal care items and home accessories made with natural or recycled materials.

Fourth World Artisans
3440 N. Southport Avenue
Chicago, IL 60657
(773) 404-5200
Hours   Tuesday through Friday 12:00 P.M. to 7:00 P.M.; Saturday 11:00 A.M. to 6:00 P.M.; Sunday 12:00 P.M. to 5:00 P.M.
A retail store where both local and international artists offer handcrafted items for sale, this storefront carries several products made from natural material as well as recycled goods. They stock hats, purses, bags, and necklaces that are constructed from hemp, sweaters that are made from recycled cotton, and quilts that are pieced together with recycled fabric. They also have toys made from recycled tin. Other items sold at this ten-year-old shop include baskets, wooden instruments (check out the didjeridu handcrafted by the aborigines of Australia), clothing from India and Indonesia, plus mudcloth from West Africa.

Grassroots
Music Box Theatre Building
3717 N. Southport Avenue
Chicago, IL 60613
(773) 248-1800
Hours   Tuesday through Friday 4:00 P.M. to 10:00 P.M.; Saturday 12:00 P.M. to 6:00 P.M.; Sunday 12:00 P.M. to 5:00 P.M.; closed Monday.

This store carries an array of clothing made with natural material such as hemp and cotton plus handmade sweaters, handbags, tapestries, and ponchos. They also sell aromatherapy soaps, candles, and incense by Nag Champa in various sizes.

The Greener Cleaner
5312 N. Broadway
Chicago, IL 60640
(773) 784-8429
Hours   Monday through Friday 7:00 A.M. to 7:00 P.M.; Saturday 8:00 A.M. to 5:00 P.M.; closed Sunday.
This strip-mall spot provides a natural alternative to dry cleaning. They don't use any of the chemicals that are used by traditional dry-cleaning establishments. Instead, the workers here clean clothes with a calogen-based product that is biodegradable and safe for the environment. With prices that are competitive with most dry-cleaning services, the Greener Cleaner is especially appealing to people who have allergies or are chemically sensitive.

Natural Resources
5949 N. Broadway
Chicago, IL 60660
(773) 878-3773
Hours   Monday through Saturday 12:00 P.M. to 6:00 P.M.; closed Sunday.
The place to go for organic tea and coffee, this storefront also stocks bulk herbs such as chamomile, alfalfa, and dandelion plus hard-to-find all-natural personal care items such as black soap and shea butter. They also have plenty of gift items for children.

Real Things
3811 N. Western Avenue
Chicago, IL 60618
(773) 588-4000

Hours   Tuesday through Saturday 12:00 P.M. to 9:00 P.M.; Sunday 1:00 P.M. to 7:00 P.M.; closed Monday.

A store filled with unique, one-of-a-kind items, this place carries hemp and 100-percent-cotton clothing. They also sell wallets made from hemp, handmade sweaters from Ecuador, tie-dyed T-shirts, patches, vests, and African statues. Medicinal herbs can also be purchased here.

Rosley's Rocks and Gems
2153 N. Sheffield Avenue
Chicago, IL 60614
(773) 868-4367
Hours   Monday, Tuesday, Thursday, Friday, and Saturday 11:00 A.M. to 6:00 P.M.; Sunday and Wednesday 12:00 P.M. to 5:00 P.M.

This metaphysical rock shop offers more than two hundred rocks, crystals, and gems, including stones from other countries such as South Africa and Brazil. Customers can buy these stones as they are or have Steve Rosley, the owner, transform them into jewelry. Rosley not only sells stones, he also offers games that include stones and crystals such as The Chakra Game and Meditation Kit. Lectures on the power of the mineral kingdom are also held at the store.

Sweet Pea Natural Toys and Gifts
3338 N. Southport Avenue
Chicago, IL 60657
(773) 281-4426
Hours   Monday through Saturday 10:00 A.M. to 6:00 P.M.; Sunday 12:00 P.M. to 5:00 P.M.

A spot that specializes in toys made of cotton, wool, and wood, this place also carries classic games such as pick-up sticks, tops, and jacks. Individuals who enjoy arts and crafts can get all-natural supplies at this storefront, including beeswax crayons, candle decorating wax, colored pencils, watercolors, 100 percent wool felt, and wooden forms for toy making. Shoppers will also find plenty of storybooks, handmade dolls, and craft kits available for sale.

Terrain
2542 N. Halsted Street
Chicago, IL 60614
(773) 549-0888
Hours   Monday through Friday 11:00 A.M. to 8:00 P.M.; Saturday 9:00 A.M. to 6:00 P.M.; Sunday 12:00 P.M. to 5:00 P.M.
This place sells their own brand of cruelty-free, botanical-based hair and skin care products plus a few aromatherapy items. They also offer other no-animal-testing brands. There's a hair salon in back of the store where stylists use products sold in the retail area.

Trés Ambiance
3335 N. Lincoln Avenue
Chicago, IL 60657
(773) 935-2121
Hours   Monday 2:00 P.M. to 8:00 P.M.; Tuesday, Wednesday, and Thursday 10:00 A.M. to 8:00 P.M.; Friday 10:00 A.M. to 6:00 P.M.; Saturday 8:00 A.M. to 2:00 P.M.; closed Sunday.
A full-service salon for clients who have sensitive skin or only use all-natural personal care products, the professionals at this place use an organic hair removal system, a hair color treatment that is botanically based, and ammonia-free perms. They also give makeup consultations using cruelty-free products.

North/Northwest Suburbs

Aveda Environmental Lifestyle Store
Northbrook Court Mall
2116 Northbrook Court
Northbrook, IL 60062
(800) 509-9354
Hours   Monday through Friday 10:00 A.M. to 9:00 P.M.; Saturday 10:00 A.M. to 7:00 P.M.; Sunday 11:00 A.M. to 6:00 P.M.
See Chicago listing for details.

Aveda Environmental Lifestyle Store
Woodfield Mall
Golf Road and Route 53
L-325
Schaumburg, IL 60173
(800) 413-0438
Hours   Monday through Friday 10:00 A.M. to 9:00 P.M.; Saturday 10:00 A.M. to 7:00 P.M.; Sunday 10:00 A.M. to 6:00 P.M.
See Chicago listing for details.

10,000 Villages
719 Main Street
Evanston, IL 60202
(847) 733-8258
Hours   Monday 10:00 A.M. to 9:00 P.M.; Tuesday through Friday 10:00 A.M. to 6:00 P.M.; Saturday 10:00 A.M. to 5:00 P.M.; closed Sunday.
This storefront stocks an array of handcrafted items made by international and local artisans. Some of these products are constructed from recycled materials and objects that might have otherwise been discarded. They carry reasonably priced jewelry such as rings made from jute and palm fiber as well as decorative pins constructed from olive wood. They also have a wide selection of natural houseware items such as palm fiber

napkin rings and placemats. Other great finds include beeswax candles and brass that isn't lacquered. Their selection of imported items is especially impressive. Don't miss the hand-carved wooden figurines and stone carvings made by craftsmen in India and Africa.

South/Southwest Suburbs

A Cottage Garden
710 N. Des Plaines Street
Plainfield, IL 60544
(815) 254-2629
Hours Tuesday through Saturday 10:00 A.M. to 6:00 P.M.; closed Sunday and Monday.
An herbal garden with a retail shop on the premises, this place offers whole herbs for sale picked fresh from the garden, such as red raspberry leaf, blessed thistle, cramp bark, feverfew, cat's claw, chickweed, and horsetail. They also have potpourri products, essential oils, herbal soaps, culinary herbs, spices, and other botanical items. Owner Diane Malone gives workshops on potpourri making and aromatherapy products and herb talks throughout the year. Tours of the garden are available during late spring and summer.

Ozone: The Environmental Store
2340 177th Street
Lansing, IL 60438
(708) 474-4077
Hours Monday through Saturday 10:00 A.M. to 6:00 P.M.; closed Sunday.
The owners of Sunrise Farm Market also own this shop, the largest environmental store in the Chicago area. Located just behind the health food store, this south suburban spot stocks clothing made from hemp, cotton, and wool. Their men's sec-

tion is particularly impressive and contains several stylish ensembles including casual shirts and dress pants made from natural material. They also carry men's and women's hemp jeans, socks, handbags, cotton bed and bath items, recycled paper supplies, personal care items, and Birkenstock shoes.

8 Organic and Vegetarian Restaurants

When my girlfriend Jessica and I find out there's a new vegetarian restaurant in town, we immediately call to make reservations. We're excited about these eating establishments for different reasons. Jessica, a budding vegetarian cook, likes to sample several of the appetizer items on the menu to see if she can duplicate them at home. I like to go because I disdain cooking and it's nice, every now and then, to have someone else prepare a hot and healthy meal for me.

The listings in this chapter include some of the discoveries we've made throughout our four-year friendship. Since I sometimes eat meat, I've included restaurants that serve some meat items as well. These restaurants use mostly organic fruits and vegetables and meats that have no preservatives, growth hormones, stimulants, antibiotics, or other chemicals.

If you've never been to a vegetarian restaurant and you'd like to visit one of the places listed in this chapter, here are a few tips before you go:

1. Take time to read the menu. Since this is your first time dining at a meatless restaurant, you want to make sure you understand just what you'll be eating. You'll see unusual words on the menu that you may have never heard of before like tempeh, seitan, and tofu. These products are

meat substitutes and allow the chefs to replicate some of the popular meat dishes sold at traditional restaurants like burgers, tacos, and barbecue.

2. Ask your waiter or waitress to describe the flavor.

3. Don't be afraid to explore. The great thing about vegetarian food is that compared to food offered at more traditional restaurants, this food is less likely to clog your arteries.

Just in case you need a little help, I've listed a few suggestions in the restaurant descriptions on the following pages.

You'll also notice that some of the restaurants indicate that a portion of their menu consists of vegan (pronounced VEE-GUN) entrées—dishes that are prepared without dairy products. Some of these restaurants are also kosher.

What you won't find in this chapter are the alternative fast food restaurants such as Pattie's and Lo•Cal Zone. These places do a good job creating scrumptious meals that are quick, nutritious, and heart-healthy, but the emphasis of this chapter is on vegetarian cooking and places that use mostly organic ingredients. Unfortunately, you won't find any listings for vegetarian or organic restaurants in the South/Southwest suburbs or the Western suburbs because, after extensive searching and checking with local vegetarian organizations, I was unable to find any. However, many area restaurants do offer vegetarian platters.

Chicago

Amitabul
3418 N. Southport Avenue
Chicago, IL 60640
(773) 472-4060
Hours   Open daily 11:00 A.M. to 10:00 P.M.
One of the newest vegetarian restaurants in the Chicago area, this spot offers traditional and alternative Korean Buddhist cuisine, which means that the food served here is totally vegan. Owner Dave Choi has named many of the entrées after customers who frequented Choi's other restaurant, Jim's Grill, named after Choi's uncle. One of the more popular dishes is called Dr. Kinsky, a spicy noodle soup made with fresh seaweed, mushrooms, bean sprouts, scallions, broccoli, turnips, and tofu. Choi claims that this soup has helped to relieve his customers of sinus problems. Another customer favorite is energy nuts, an array of vegetables such as broccoli, zucchini, radishes, bean sprouts, scallions, nuts, and noodles served over brown rice. For dessert, try the rice cake made with sweet red beans. Choi teaches vegetarian cooking classes at various places throughout the city and offers a healthy eating program that involves one or two prepared meals a day for an entire month. This regimen is designed to change metabolism and detoxify the body. The entrées at this place are inexpensive; all dishes are under $8.

Blind Faith Café
3300 N. Lincoln Avenue
Chicago, IL 60657
(773) 871-3820
Hours   Monday through Thursday 11:00 A.M. to 10:00 P.M.; Friday 11:00 A.M. to 11:00 P.M.; Saturday 9:00 A.M. to 11:00 P.M.; Sunday 9:00 A.M. to 10:00 P.M.

A charming restaurant where families frequently dine, this place offers a variety of vegetarian dishes including such favorites as Hoisen Tempeh, Bi Bim Bop (a seitan dish cooked up like a stir-fry with a sweet-tasting sauce), Macrobiotic Plate, Chili Enchiladas, and Tempeh Patty Sandwich. Most items can be made vegan-style when requested. The restaurant in Chicago is the newer location and has been open since 1997. There's a self-service area at the Evanston spot for patrons who want a quick bite to eat and a bakery that offers a wide variety of desserts including whole wheat muffins and some low-fat, sugarless items. The bakery in Evanston is open Sunday through Wednesday 10:00 A.M. to 4:00 P.M. and Thursday through Saturday 10:00 A.M. to 7:00 P.M. The average price for an entrée is $9.

Charlie Trotter's
816 W. Armitage Avenue
Chicago, IL 60614
(773) 248-6228
Hours   Tuesday through Saturday 6:00 P.M. to 10:00 P.M.; closed Sunday and Monday.
This is one of Chicago's most exclusive restaurants. Internationally acclaimed chef Charlie Trotter uses organic produce in several of the dishes served at his restaurant because of its delicious, wholesome flavor. He also uses free-range meats. The vegetarian degustations are $85; the regular degustations are $95. Valet parking is available. Reservations are required.

The Chicago Diner
3411 N. Halsted Street
Chicago, IL 60614
(773) 935-6696
Hours   Monday through Friday 11:00 A.M. to 10:00 P.M.; Saturday and Sunday 10:00 A.M. to 10:00 P.M.
A popular hangout for naturals, this restaurant offers a variety of hearty and healthy meals on their mostly vegan menu, such

as the Country Pot Pie (made with chunks of tofu), Future Burger (a baked grainburger served on a seven-grain bun), Fiery Fajitas, and Big Salad. The Chicago Diner is also known for its delicious dairy-free desserts such as cheesecakes that come in various flavors like blueberry, strawberry, and peach; sugar-free cookies; and muffins. You can also buy their guilt-less dessert items in the bakery section of some Whole Foods markets. Prices of entrées range from $6 to $9.

Earth
738 N. Wells Street
Chicago, IL 60610
(312) 335-5475
Hours Monday through Saturday 11:30 A.M. to 2:30 P.M. (lunch); Tuesday through Thursday 5:30 P.M. to 9:00 P.M. (dinner); Friday and Saturday 5:30 P.M. to 10:00 P.M. (dinner); closed Sunday.
What's great about this restaurant is that it appeals to both meat eaters and vegetarians. Their lunch menu features a variety of exotic salads including the Earth Salad, which consists of baby greens, spinach, cucumber, radish, garbanzo beans, tomatoes, and other vegetables. They also serve an array of soups and a nice mixture of meat and meatless sandwiches. Their dinner menu is just as diverse and includes such favorites as the Vegetable Strudel with Shrimp (also available without shrimp); Jungle Curry with Tofu, Vegetables, Coconut Milk, Basil, Lime Leaf, and Thai Fish Sauce; and Lemon Herb Roast Chicken with Mashed Potatoes and Natural Jus. The chef at this place uses organic vegetables and meat that is free of growth hormones. They also offer freshly squeezed juices and organic beer and wine. Not only is the food free of pesticides and other chemicals, but the interior of the restaurant is environmentally friendly, too. The walls are decorated with paints and finishes free of organic compounds, the tabletops are constructed from formaldehyde-free material, and the floor is made of sustain-

ably harvested wood. The entrées at this place range from $6 to $9 for lunch and $8 to $18 for dinner.

eden, the natural bistro
1000 W. North Avenue, Second Floor
Chicago, IL 60622
(312) 587-3060
Hours   Monday through Friday 11:30 A.M. to 9:00 P.M.; Saturday 11:00 A.M. to 9:00 P.M.; Sunday 11:00 A.M. to 5:00 P.M.
Going grocery shopping? You can also get a good hot meal when you shop at the Whole Foods Market on North Avenue. The second floor of this mega health food store contains a restaurant serving food that is free of pesticides, preservatives, artificial flavors, sweeteners, growth hormones, and other chemicals. In other words, it's all organic. Menu items include meat and meatless dishes such as Curried Chicken, Red Beans and Rice, Sun Dried Tomato and Artichoke Pasta, and Free Roam Chicken Stir-Fry. Try the Baked Wild Mushroom Phyllo Rolls as an appetizer and a cup of corn chowder for a quick bite. The menu also contains some vegan items. Entrées range from $7 to $13.

foodlife
Water Tower Place
835 N. Michigan Avenue
Chicago, IL 60611
(312) 335-3663
Hours   Friday and Saturday 11:00 A.M. to 10:00 P.M.; Sunday through Thursday 11:00 A.M. to 8:00 P.M.
Located on the mezzanine level of Water Tower Place, this Rich Melman spot is a natural food cafeteria rather than a sit-down restaurant. Customers can choose entrées from thirteen kitchens and all of them offer good-for-you food items such as stir-fry dishes, sugar-free desserts, and an organic juice bar. The Food for Life station offers vegetarian meals including an

array of salads, beans, and rice. Price for a meal, including beverage, ranges from $10 to $15.

The Heartland Café
7000 N. Glenwood Avenue
Chicago, IL 60626
(773) 465-8005
Hours   Monday through Thursday 7:00 A.M. to 11:00 P.M.; Friday 7:00 A.M. to 11:00 P.M.; Saturday 8:00 A.M. to 11:00 P.M.; Sunday 8:00 A.M. to 10:00 P.M.
One of the first vegetarian restaurants in the city, this twenty-two-year-old spot consists of a restaurant, general store, bar, and theater. The entrées on the menu appeal to meat eaters and vegetarians as well as individuals following a vegan or macrobiotic diet. Some of their specialties include the Vegetarian Chili served with hot corn bread, Mexican Chicken accompanied with rice and beans plus steamed vegetables, the Buffalo Burger, and the Seitan Fajitas. The chefs bake their own bread and make their own pies. Try the apple cobbler for dessert. Owner Michael James says they use organic produce whenever they can and the meat served is farm-raised. In addition to alcoholic beverages—check out the restaurant's Red Line Tap—they also have an organic juice bar. "We serve everything from carrot juice to Cuervo," James says. The entrées range from $5 to $13.

Jim's Grill
1429 W. Irving Park Road
Chicago, IL 60640
(773) 525-4050
Hours   Monday through Saturday 7:00 A.M. to 3:30 P.M.; closed Sunday.
A small diner that's open only for breakfast and lunch, this place serves vegetarian and nonvegetarian meals. It also offers some vegan items. Their specialty is the Bi Bim Bop, a Korean

dish which is an assortment of vegetables served over white or brown rice. The Vegetarian Pancakes are another popular entrée and are made with whole wheat flour and vegetables such as zucchini, sweet potatoes, and carrots topped with a syrup made of plum sauce and brown rice miso. Nonvegetarians will enjoy the Korean Omelet. Prices are very reasonable; none of the entrées are over $6.

Karyn's Fresh Corner
3351 N. Lincoln Avenue
Chicago, IL 60657
Hours   Monday through Friday 11:00 A.M. to 9:00 P.M.; Saturday and Sunday 10:00 A.M. to 9:00 P.M.
You'll feel light as a feather after eating at this spot enjoyed by diners who appreciate the rich, unadulterated flavor of raw food. Although this all-vegan restaurant offers some cooked food, 85 percent of the menu contains raw food entrées. Some favorites are the gazpacho, a cold soup consisting of a medley of fresh tomatoes, onions, garlic, zucchini, and red and yellow peppers. The Raw Pasta is not raw noodles but raw zucchini shredded like pasta and served with a pesto sauce made with pine nuts, sun dried tomatoes, onions, garlic, and olive oil. The Raw Pizza is another favorite and is made with a dehydrated crust of sprouted wheat berries topped with marinated eggplant, mushrooms, sprouts, and carrots. For dessert, try the Raw German Chocolate Cake made with sprouted wheat berries, fresh coconut, vanilla, and dates with a nondairy carob frosting. Entrées range from $5 to $10. If you want to try a sampling of both raw and cooked food items, order the All You Can Eat Buffet, offered daily for $10. Owner Karyn Calabrese counsels people on the benefits of raw foods and gives workshops regarding healthy eating at this location or at her holistic health-care facility, Karyn's Inner Beauty Center. (See Chapter 1 for information on this store.)

Mother Earth Café and Organic Juice Bar
2570 N. Lincoln Avenue
Chicago, IL 60614
(773) 327-8459
Hours   Monday through Friday 11:00 A.M. to 8:00 P.M.; Saturday 10:00 A.M. to 8:00 P.M.; Sunday 12:00 P.M. to 6:00 P.M.
A favorite meeting place for the New Age crowd, this café, which is tucked neatly inside Healing Earth Resource Center (see Chapter 4 for information on this center), offers an array of quick vegetarian entrées at very reasonable prices. A cup of soup starts at $3 and comes with a choice of rice, toast, or corn bread. Their herb lentil loaf is a favorite as are their meatless burger sandwiches. I love their barbecue burger that is made with soy. Prices range from $3 to $8.

Reza's Restaurant
432 W. Ontario Street
Chicago, IL 60610
(312) 664-4500
5255 N. Clark Street
Chicago, IL 60640
(773) 561-1898
Hours   Open daily 11:00 A.M. to 12:00 A.M.
Another place that caters to both carnivores and vegetarians, this restaurant has two locations in the city and offers a variety of creative Persian, Mediterranean, and vegetarian meals. Meat eaters can choose from entrées made with beef, fish, poultry, and lamb while vegetarians can select from twenty-three appetizers plus a moderate selection of lunch and dinner items. Can't decide what to eat? Try anything on the menu with grilled mushrooms, hummus, or tabouli. The price of an entrée ranges from $6 to $10 for lunch and $7 to $15 for dinner.

Soul Vegetarian
205 E. 75th Street
Chicago, IL 60619
(773) 224-0104
Hours   Monday 9:00 A.M. to 9:00 P.M.; Tuesday through Thursday 11:00 A.M. to 10:00 P.M.; Friday 11:00 A.M. to 11:00 P.M.; Saturday 9:00 A.M. to 11:00 P.M.; Sunday 9:00 A.M. to 8:00 P.M.
Owned by the African Hebrew Israelites of Jerusalem, this South Side restaurant serves down-home cooking with a vegetarian flair. Although all meals are meatless, they taste like the real thing. Some of their lip-smacking entrées include corn, greens, and potato salad without dairy ingredients. There's also the Garvey Burger, Barbecue Delight, and Barbecue Twist—mock barbecue ribs—and, for dessert, soybean ice cream. The entrées at this place are truly food for the vegan soul! All menu items are kosher. Prices range from $3 to $8.

Vegetarian Garden
237 W. Cermak Road
Chicago, IL 60616
(312) 949-1388
Hours   Wednesday through Monday 10:30 A.M. to 10:30 P.M.; closed Tuesday.
This place serves Chinese food that is both kosher and vegan. Entrées are prepared without MSG and include Mongolian Beef made with seitan and General Tso's Chicken made with tofu. Other favorites are the Vegetable Sausage and Singapore Stir-fry Noodles, for those who like their food hot and spicy. Entrées range from $7 to $9.

North/Northwest Suburbs

Blind Faith Café
525 Dempster Street
Evanston, IL 60201
(847) 328-6875
Hours   Sunday through Thursday 10:00 A.M. to 9:00 P.M.; Friday and Saturday 10:00 A.M. to 10:00 P.M. (self-service area); Monday through Thursday 11:00 A.M. to 9:00 P.M.; Friday 11:00 A.M. to 10:00 P.M.; Saturday 10:00 A.M. to 10:00 P.M.; Sunday 10:00 A.M. to 9:00 P.M. (restaurant).
See Chicago listing for description.

The Chicago Diner
581 Elm Place
Highland Park, IL 60035
(847) 433-1228
Hours   Tuesday through Friday 11:00 A.M. to 3:00 P.M. (lunch) and 5:00 P.M. to 9:00 P.M. (dinner); Saturday 11:00 A.M. to 10:00 P.M.; Sunday 11:00 A.M. to 8:00 P.M.; closed Monday.
See Chicago listing for description.

Chowpatti Vegetarian Restaurant
1035 S. Arlington Heights Road
Arlington Heights, IL 60005
(847) 640-9554
Hours   Tuesday through Thursday 11:30 A.M. to 9:00 P.M.; Friday and Saturday 11:30 A.M. to 10:00 P.M.; closed Monday.
This family-owned restaurant has a twenty-page menu full of different types of vegetarian cuisine including American, Italian, Mexican, Middle Eastern, and Indian entrées. A few customer favorites are the Chowpatti Veggie Burger, Veggie Lasgna, Veggie Quesadilla, Sev Batata Puri (Indian nachos), and falafel. Only a few food items can be made wheat-free, but most can be prepared vegan. The waitstaff is easygoing

and won't rush you from tables. Prices of entrées range from $5 to $10.

Slice of Life
4120 Dempster Avenue
Skokie, IL 60076
(847) 674-2021
Hours   Monday through Thursday 11:30 A.M. to 9:00 P.M.; Friday 11:30 A.M. to 2:00 P.M.; Saturday ninety minutes after sundown to 1:00 A.M.; Sunday 10:30 A.M. to 9:00 P.M.
A kosher vegetarian restaurant, this place serves some vegan dishes as well as a few fish entrées. The Seitan Sandwich, Pasta Caesario, and quesadillas are just a few customer favorites. Their nondairy desserts are delicious and include German chocolate cake and chocolate cream pie. They also have a children's menu. Entrées range from $6 to $20.

9 Groups and Publications

In the foreword of this book, Dr. Bruno Cortis predicts that the physician's role in the patient/physician relationship will soon change. He predicts that physicians will begin putting more emphasis on treating the patient rather than the disease and that an increasing number of health-care physicians will begin working in partnership with their patients to achieve good health. It's good to know that your journey to wellness does not have to be a solitary affair. But there are other people besides your personal physician who can give you guidance on ways to improve your health.

This chapter contains the names of groups you can join that will either provide information on alternative health care or assist you during your quest to live a more natural lifestyle. Some of the groups I've listed, such as the Cancer Prevention Coalition, are politically involved and actively lobby for change. Other groups focus solely on providing information. This chapter also contains a list of local publications that describe alternative health-related events occurring in the area.

What this chapter does not contain are national organizations and groups that are well-known by the public that support people who are stricken with life-threatening diseases such as cancer and AIDS. The resources that are listed are small, local groups that emphasize preventive medicine and alternative health care as a method of healing. I've also listed a few resources that reflect a concern for the well-being of the earth.

Groups

Angelic Organics
1547 Rockton Road
Caledonia, IL 61011
(312) 409-2746
This is a Vegetable of the Week Club. Members or subscribers of this community-supported agriculture group receive a weekly box of this biodynamic farm's freshest, seasonal, organic produce from late June through the middle of November. Some of the crops include beans, cucumbers, sweet corn, winter squash, kale, mustard greens, basil, parsley, cabbage, onions, beets, and potatoes. There's also a special selection of produce for those who are following a macrobiotic diet. Members are required to pick up their shipments at one of the twelve delivery sites in the Chicago area.

Blooming Prairie
Buying Club Coordinator
2340 Heinz Road
Iowa City, IA 52240
(800) 323-2131
(319) 337-6448
This distributor maintains a list of natural food-buying clubs located in the Chicago area. Blooming Prairie supplies these groups with various natural food items. The members are able to save money on items that are typically sold in health food stores since they buy directly from the distributor. Members meet at a central location where the delivery truck drops off

cases of products. They're responsible for unloading the truck and distributing the products among their members. The items are usually paid for in advance. To find a group near your home or to organize one in your area, call Blooming Prairie.

Cancer Prevention Coalition
c/o Dr. Samuel S. Epstein
School of Public Health
2121 W. Taylor Street
Chicago, IL 60612
(312) 996-2297
A nonprofit, educational, and advocacy organization, this group's mission is to implement community-based solutions for the reduction of avoidable cancer risks. They also present programs to increase awareness and stimulate action for cancer prevention.

Chicago Vegetarian Society
c/o Kay Stepkin
P.O. Box 578995
Chicago, IL 60657
(773) 975-VEGY
This group meets on a monthly basis at different restaurants or group members' homes to sample vegetarian cuisine. Membership includes a newsletter.

Multiple Chemical Sensitivities: Health & Environment
c/o Lynn Lawson
P.O. Box 1732
Evanston, IL 60201
(630) 529-1342
A support group for people who are chemically sensitive or have been diagnosed with an environment-related illness, this group sponsors lecturers who speak on various aspects of environmental health. The membership fee is $20 and includes their national bimonthly newsletter *CanaryNews*.

Northwest Vegetarians
c/o Maahesh Shah
164 Springwood Lane
Barrington, IL 60010
(847) 836-6246
This group meets monthly to enjoy vegetarian dishes and the camaraderie of other people with similar interests.

Nutrition for Optimal Health Association
P.O. Box 380
Winnetka, IL 60093
(708) 786-5326
This organization sponsors a lecture series on preventive health from September through May. Membership is $35 and includes a subscription to their newsletter.

South Suburban Food Co-op
21750 Main Street
Matteson, IL 60443
(708) 747-2256
This is the only consumer cooperative of its kind in the Chicago area. Members of this group get a price reduction on organic food and other health food items in exchange for two hours of work each month at their private health food store located in a warehouse. Work requirements are waived for senior citizens. A small membership fee is required each year.

Will County Vegetarian Society
c/o Lasting Images Art & Frame Shop
Cindy Notter
2080 E. Division Street
Coal City, IL 60416
(815) 634-8198
This far South/Southwest suburban group meets monthly for socializing and sharing of food and recipes with other members.

Publications

Conscious Choice: The Journal of Ecology & Natural Living
Conscious Communications, Inc.
920 N. Franklin Street, Suite 202
Chicago, IL 60610
(312) 440-4373
Distributed free in natural food markets, health food stores, and some bookstores in the city and suburbs, this publication is one of the best resources in the area on holistic health and living. It contains articles on ecology, nutrition, and alternative health care. Published six times a year, a subscription to this magazine is $27 first-class mail or $18 third-class mail.

Holistic Chicago
Holistic America, Inc.
711 W. Lake Street, Suite 603
Minneapolis, MN 55408
(612) 825-6644
Another free publication, this bimonthly magazine is distributed in the city and the North/Northwest and Western suburbs at a number of outlets including natural food markets, health food stores, holistic health-care facilities, and bookstores. This publication lists holistic health-care providers and other health-related resources in the Chicago area, contains articles on various aspects of holistic health and living, and lists a calendar of events. Home delivery is available through subscription for $18 a year.

The Monthly Aspectarian
Lightworks Communications, Inc.
P.O. Box 1342
Morton Grove, IL 60053
(847) 966-1110

Now in its twentieth year, this Chicago-area New Age magazine started out as an advertising vehicle of sorts and then evolved into a magazine. It contains articles on astrology, spirituality, and holistic health care. It also reports on the latest alternative health-care events in the area. Although copies of this publication are distributed free at some natural food markets and metaphysical bookstores, you can have this delivered to your home for $36 a year.

YogaChicago
c/o OmniType
372 W. Ontario Street, Suite 301
Chicago, IL 60610
(312) 280-9011
This bimonthly publication is a resource guide of yoga activities in the Chicago area and is distributed free in bookstores, natural food stores, holistic health centers, libraries, park buildings, colleges, and learning centers throughout Chicago and its suburbs. A one-year subscription is $15.

Newsletters

The Natural Pharmacist
c/o Naturally Speaking
P.O. Box 4080
Joliet, IL 60434
(815) 439-1442
A quarterly newsletter written by Alison Lapinski, R.Ph., this publication educates readers on the benefits of natural remedies. In almost every issue, the author, a pharmacist who studied Western and Chinese herbology, compares and contrasts popular pharmaceutical remedies with Chinese or Western herbal preparations. Lapinski, of course, is in favor of most all-natural remedies, but advises that you discuss your choice to follow a natural health program with your doctor. There's also a column in the newsletter entitled "Ask the Pharmacist" that gives readers a chance to ask questions about herbs and how they compare with pharmaceutical products. A year's subscription to this newsletter is $30.

NOHA News
Nutrition for Optimal Health Association, Inc.
P.O. Box 380
Winnetka, IL 60093
This newsletter contains information on preventive medicine and nutrition. Published four times a year, the subscription fee is $8.

Appendix A

Abbreviations of Professional Credentials

C.C.H.T.	Certified Clinical Hypnotherapist
D.A.C.B.N.	Diplomat of the American Chiropractic Board of Nutrition
D.C.	Doctor of Chiropractic
D.D.S.	Doctor of Dental Science
D.M.D.	Doctor of Medical Dentistry
D.N.	Doctor of Naprapathy
D.N.B.H.E.	Diplomat of the National Board of Homeopathic Examiners
D.O.	Doctor of Osteopathy
D.Sc.	Doctor of Science
D.V.M.	Doctor of Veterinary Medicine
F.A.C.C.	Fellow of American College of Cardiology
L.C.P.C.	Licensed Clinical Professional Counselor
L.C.S.W.	Licensed Clinical Social Worker or Licensed Certified Social Worker
M.A.	Master of Arts (Ask the practitioner to identify which field.)
M.D.	Doctor of Medicine
M.E.D.	Master of Education Degree
M.H.D.	Doctorate in Complementary Medicine
M.P.H.	Master of Public Health
M.S.W.	Master of Social Work
MT-BC	Music Therapist–Board Certified
N.D.	Doctor of Naturopathy
Ph.D.	Doctor of Philosophy (Ask the practitioner to identify which field.)
R.H.D.	Rohun Doctorate
R.N.	Registered Nurse
R.Ph.	Registered Pharmacist

Certification Information

The holistic practitioners that are listed in this book have obtained certifications from various sources including accredited educational institutions, certified schools of technique or training programs, and professional organizations. Some practitioners have even had long-standing apprenticeship programs with masters of a specific healing modality. Although I have taken extreme measures to ensure that the practitioners in this book have obtained the appropriate certifications, I encourage you to ask practitioners about their qualifications.

You should know that although there are no massage practice laws in the state of Illinois, some massage therapists in the city of Chicago are licensed by the city to practice massage therapy; however, practitioners, whether they practice massage in the city or suburbs, should have some kind of training. Ask the practitioner if he or she was trained at a school that has the accreditation of the Commission on Massage Therapy Accreditation (COMTA). COMTA was created by the American Massage Therapy Association, which is the oldest and largest professional group of body workers in the country.

The health professionals that are listed in the book, such as chiropractors, medical doctors, dentists, psychologists, and doctors of osteopathy, are licensed by the state of Illinois to practice medicine. At present, the use of acupuncture is legal in Illinois; however, there is no agreement on how these practitioners should identify themselves in the marketplace. Some practitioners in the Chicago area are licensed in the state of Wisconsin and some use the acronym L.Ac. to denote their expertise. The listed acupuncturists are either board certified or have attended an accredited school of acupuncture.

Appendix B

Chain Store Locations in Chicago and the Suburbs

See Chapter 2 for a description of General Nutrition Center (GNC). See Chapter 6 for a descriptions of the Mario Tricoci spa experience. See Chapter 7 for descriptions of Bath & Body Works, The Body Shop, Crabtree & Evelyn, and Garden Botanika.

Chicago

Bath & Body Works
29 S. Wabash Avenue
Chicago, IL 60603
(312) 263-6780
Hours   Monday through Friday 10:00 A.M. to 6:00 P.M.; Saturday 10:00 A.M. to 5:00 P.M.; Sunday 11:00 A.M. to 4:00 P.M.

Bath & Body Works
Chicago Ridge Mall
350 Chicago Ridge
Chicago, IL 60415
(708) 636-6853
Hours   Monday through Friday 10:00 a.m. to 9:00 p.m.; Saturday 10:00 a.m. to 7:00 p.m.; Sunday 11:00 a.m. to 6:00 p.m.

Bath & Body Works
Citicorp Center
500 W. Madison Avenue
Chicago, IL 60661
(312) 466-8837
Hours   Monday through Friday 7:00 A.M. to 6:30 P.M.; Saturday 12:00 P.M. to 4:00 P.M.; closed Sunday.

Bath & Body Works
Ford City Mall
7601 S. Cicero Street
Chicago, IL 60652
(773) 581-5832
Hours   Monday through Saturday 10:00 A.M. to 9:00 P.M.; Sunday 11:00 A.M. to 6:00 P.M.

Bath & Body Works
Water Tower Place
835 N. Michigan Avenue
Chicago, IL 60611
(312) 751-1880
Hours   Monday through Thursday 10:00 A.M. to 7:00 P.M.; Friday 10:00 A.M. to 8:00 P.M.; Saturday 10:00 A.M. to 6:00 P.M.; Sunday 12:00 P.M. to 6:00 P.M.

The Body Shop
Chicago Place
700 N. Michigan Avenue
Chicago, IL 60611
(312) 482-8301
Hours   Monday through Friday 10:00 A.M. to 7:00 P.M.; Saturday 11:00 A.M. to 6:00 P.M.; Sunday 12:00 P.M. to 5:00 P.M.

Crabtree & Evelyn
634 N. Michigan Avenue
Chicago, IL 60611
(312) 944-4707
Hours   (January through May) Monday through Saturday 10:00 A.M. to 6:00 P.M.; Sunday 12:00 P.M. to 5:00 P.M.; (June through December) Monday through Friday 10:00 A.M. to 7:00 P.M.; Saturday 10:00 A.M. to 6:00 P.M.; Sunday 12:00 P.M. to 5:00 P.M.

Crabtree & Evelyn
Merchandise Mart Plaza
222 Merchandise Plaza
Space 1460
Chicago, IL 60654
(312) 644-5551
Hours   Monday through Friday 9:00 A.M. to 6:00 P.M.; Saturday 10:00 A.M. to 5:00 P.M.; closed Sunday.

Crabtree & Evelyn
Water Tower Place
835 N. Michigan Avenue
Chicago, IL 60611
(312) 787-0188
Hours   Monday through Thursday 10:00 A.M. to 7:00 P.M.; Friday 10:00 A.M. to 8:00 P.M.; Saturday 10:00 A.M. to 6:00 P.M.; Sunday 12:00 P.M. to 6:00 P.M.

Garden Botanika
2058 N. Halsted Street
Chicago, IL 60614
(773) 388-0200
Hours   Monday through Saturday 10:00 A.M. to 6:00 P.M.; Sunday 11:00 A.M. to 5:00 P.M.

Garden Botanika
Water Tower Place
835 N. Michigan Avenue
Chicago, IL 60611
(312) 397-1914
Hours   Monday through Thursday 10:00 A.M. to 7:00 P.M.; Friday 10:00 A.M. to 8:00 P.M.; Saturday 10:00 A.M. to 6:00 P.M.; Sunday 12:00 P.M. to 6:00 P.M.

General Nutrition Center
Addison Mall
2937 W. Addison Street
Chicago, IL 60618
(773) 267-8612

Hours Monday through Friday 10:00 A.M. to 9:00 P.M.; Saturday 10:00 A.M. to 5:00 P.M.; Sunday 11:00 A.M. to 5:00 P.M.

General Nutrition Center
Atrium Mall
100 W. Randolph Drive
Chicago, IL 60601
(312) 269-5980
Hours Monday through Friday 8:00 A.M. to 6:00 P.M.; closed Saturday and Sunday.

General Nutrition Center
Brickyard Mall
6465 W. Diversey Avenue
Chicago, IL 60707
(773) 637-3811
Hours Monday through Saturday 10:00 A.M. to 9:00 P.M.; Sunday 11:00 A.M. to 6:00 P.M.

General Nutrition Center
Ford City Shopping Center
7601 S. Cicero Avenue
Chicago, IL 60652
(312) 581-3325
Hours Monday through Friday 10:00 A.M. to 9:00 P.M.; Saturday 10:00 A.M. to 7:00 P.M.; Sunday 11:00 A.M. to 6:00 P.M.

General Nutrition Center
Merchandise Mart
222 Merchandise Mart Plaza
Space 126
Chicago, IL 60654
(312) 832-6990
Hours Monday through Friday 9:00 A.M. to 6:00 P.M.; Saturday 10:00 A.M. to 5:00 P.M.; closed Sunday.

General Nutrition Center
River Point Shopping Center
1730 W. Fullerton Avenue
Chicago, IL 60614
(773) 281-6672
Hours Monday through Friday 10:00 A.M. to 9:00 P.M.; Saturday 10:00 A.M. to 6:00 P.M.; Sunday 11:00 A.M. to 5:00 P.M.

General Nutrition Center
Town Center
3333 W. Touhy Avenue
Chicago, IL 60645
(847) 674-5999
Hours Monday through Friday 10:00 A.M. to 9:00 P.M.; Saturday 10:00 A.M. to 6:00 P.M.; Sunday 11:00 A.M. to 6:00 P.M.

General Nutrition Center
1519 E. 53rd Street
Chicago, IL 60615
(773) 493-1564
Hours Monday through Saturday 10:00 A.M. to 5:30 P.M.; Sunday 12:00 P.M. to 4:30 P.M.

General Nutrition Center
5240 N. Pulaski Road
Chicago, IL 60630
(773) 463-5516
Hours   Monday through Friday 10:00 A.M. to 8:00 P.M.; Saturday 10:00 A.M. to 6:00 P.M.; Sunday 11:00 A.M. to 5:00 P.M.

General Nutrition Center
4836 Irving Park Road
Chicago, IL 60641
(773) 685-0118
Hours   Monday through Friday 10:00 A.M. to 5:30 P.M.; Saturday 10:00 A.M. to 5:00 P.M.; Sunday 12:00 P.M. to 5:00 P.M.

General Nutrition Center
2740 N. Clark Street
Chicago, IL 60614
(773) 528-7887
Hours   Monday through Friday 10:00 A.M. to 9:00 P.M.; Saturday 10:00 A.M. to 7:00 P.M.; Sunday 11:00 A.M. to 6:00 P.M.

General Nutrition Center
33 N. Dearborn Street
Chicago, IL 60602
(312) 357-0903
Hours   Monday through Friday 8:00 A.M. to 6:00 P.M.; Saturday 10:00 A.M. to 3:00 P.M.; closed Sunday.

General Nutrition Center
174 N. Wabash Avenue
Chicago, IL 60601
(312) 368-4558
Hours   Monday through Friday 8:00 A.M. to 6:00 P.M.; Saturday 10:00 A.M. to 4:00 P.M.; closed Sunday.

General Nutrition Center
244 S. State Street
Chicago, IL 60604
(312) 967-9885
Hours   Monday through Friday 8:00 A.M. to 6:00 P.M.; Saturday 10:00 A.M. to 4:00 P.M.; closed Sunday.

General Nutrition Center
5616 W. Belmont Avenue
Chicago, IL 60634
(773) 685-0243
Hours   Monday, Tuesday, and Wednesday 10:00 A.M. to 5:30 P.M.; Thursday 10:00 A.M. to 8:00 P.M.; Friday 10:00 A.M. to 5:30 P.M.; Saturday 10:00 A.M. to 5:30 P.M.; Sunday 12:00 P.M. to 5:00 P.M.

General Nutrition Center
164 W. Division Street
Chicago, IL 60610
(312) 266-2743
Hours   Monday through Friday

10:00 A.M. to 7:00 P.M.; Saturday 10:00 A.M. to 6:00 P.M.; closed Sunday.

General Nutrition Center
7 W. Madison Street
Chicago, IL 60602
(312) 759-0638
Hours   Monday through Friday 8:00 A.M. to 6:00 P.M.; Saturday 10:00 A.M. to 3:00 P.M.; closed Sunday.

General Nutrition Center
174 N. Michigan Avenue
Chicago, IL 60602
(312) 357-6512
Hours   Monday through Friday 8:00 A.M. to 6:00 P.M.; Saturday 10:00 A.M. to 5:00 P.M.; closed Sunday.

General Nutrition Center
1281 W. Milwaukee Avenue
Chicago, IL 60622
(773) 227-1388
Hours   Monday through Friday 10:00 A.M. to 6:00 P.M.; Saturday 10:00 A.M. to 5:00 P.M.; Sunday 11:00 A.M. to 5:00 P.M.

General Nutrition Center
22 W. Monroe Street
Chicago, IL 60603
(312) 419-8839

Hours   Monday through Friday 8:00 A.M. to 6:00 P.M.; Saturday 10:00 A.M. to 3:00 P.M.; closed Sunday.

North/Northwest Suburbs

Bath & Body Works
Highland Park Mall
661 Central Avenue
Highland Park, IL 60035
(847) 266-8027
Hours   Monday through Friday 9:30 A.M. to 6:00 P.M.; Saturday 11:00 A.M. to 5:00 P.M.; closed Sunday.

Bath & Body Works
Lincolnwood Town Center
3333 W. Touhy Avenue
Lincolnwood, IL 60645
(847) 674-9950
Hours   Monday through Friday 10:00 A.M. to 9:00 P.M.; Saturday 10:00 A.M. to 7:00 P.M.; Sunday 11:00 A.M. to 6:00 P.M.

Bath & Body Works
Randhurst Mall
999 N. Elmhurst Road
Mount Prospect, IL 60056
(847) 253-9130
Hours   Monday through Friday 10:00 A.M. to 9:00 P.M.; Saturday 10:00 A.M. to 7:00 P.M.; Sunday 11:00 A.M. to 6:00 P.M.

Bath & Body Works
Golf Mill Shopping Center
239 Golf Mill Road
Niles, IL 60714
(847) 390-0980
Hours   Monday through Saturday 10:00 A.M. to 9:00 P.M.; Sunday 11:00 A.M. to 6:00 P.M.

Bath & Body Works
Northbrook Court
1304 Northbrook Court
Northbrook, IL 60062
(847) 498-1050
Hours   Monday through Friday 10:00 A.M. to 9:00 P.M.; Saturday 10:00 A.M. to 7:00 P.M.; Sunday 11:00 A.M. to 6:00 P.M.

Bath & Body Works
Woodfield Mall
Space E-134
Schaumburg, IL 60173
(847) 413-8526
Hours   Monday through Friday 10:00 A.M. to 9:00 P.M.; Saturday 10:00 A.M. to 7:00 P.M.; Sunday 11:00 A.M. to 6:00 P.M.

Bath & Body Works
Old Orchard Shopping Center
153 Old Orchard Center
Skokie, IL 60077
(847) 677-6745

Hours   Monday through Friday 10:00 A.M. to 9:00 P.M.; Saturday 10:00 A.M. to 7:00 P.M.; Sunday 11:00 A.M. to 6:00 P.M.

Bath & Body Works
Hawthorne Center
706 Hawthorne Center
Vernon Hills, IL 60061
(847) 816-3740
Hours   Monday through Friday 10:00 A.M. to 9:00 P.M.; Saturday 10:00 A.M. to 7:00 P.M.; Sunday 11:00 A.M. to 6:00 P.M.

Bath & Body Works
Spring Hill Mall
1242 Spring Hill Mall
West Dundee, IL 60118
(847) 426-3745
Hours   Monday through Friday 10:00 A.M. to 9:00 P.M.; Saturday 10:00 A.M. to 7:00 P.M.; Sunday 11:00 A.M. to 6:00 P.M.

The Body Shop
Northbrook Court
2248 Northbrook Court
Northbrook, IL 60062
(847) 559-9122
Hours   Monday through Friday 10:00 A.M. to 9:00 P.M.; Saturday 10:00 A.M. to 7:00 P.M.; Sunday 11:00 A.M. to 7:00 P.M.

The Body Shop
Woodfield Mall
Space F-322
Schaumburg, IL 60173
(847) 619-1719
Hours   Monday through Friday
10:00 A.M. to 9:00 P.M.; Saturday
10:00 A.M. to 7:00 P.M.; Sunday
11:00 A.M. to 6:00 P.M.

The Body Shop
Old Orchard Shopping Center
350 Old Orchard Center
Skokie, IL 60077
(847) 679-1970
Hours   Monday through Friday
10:00 A.M. to 9:00 P.M.; Saturday
10:00 A.M. to 7:00 P.M.; Sunday
11:00 A.M. to 6:00 P.M.

Crabtree & Evelyn
Woodfield Mall Space L-27
Schaumburg, IL 60173
(847) 330-0724
Hours   Monday through Friday
10:00 A.M. to 9:00 P.M.; Saturday
10:00 A.M. to 7:00 P.M.; Sunday
11:00 A.M. to 6:00 P.M.

Crabtree & Evelyn
Old Orchard Shopping Center
235 Old Orchard Center
Skokie, IL 60077
(847) 675-1120
Hours   Monday through Friday
10:00 A.M. to 9:00 P.M.; Saturday
10:00 A.M. to 7:00 P.M.; Sunday
11:00 A.M. to 6:00 P.M.

Crabtree & Evelyn
Hawthorne Center
216 Hawthorne Center
Vernon Hills, IL 60061
(847) 549-7901
Hours   Monday through Friday
10:00 A.M. to 9:00 P.M.; Saturday
10:00 A.M. to 7:00 P.M.; Sunday
11:00 A.M. to 6:00 P.M.

Garden Botanika
Old Orchard Shopping Center
235 Old Orchard Center
Skokie, IL 60077
(847) 675-2725
Hours   Monday through Friday
10:00 A.M. to 9:30 P.M.; Saturday
10:00 A.M. to 7:00 P.M.; Sunday
11:00 A.M. to 6:00 P.M.

Garden Botanika
Hawthorne Center
622 Hawthorne Center
Vernon Hills, IL 60061
(847) 816-3853
Hours   Monday through Friday
10:00 A.M. to 9:00 P.M.; Saturday
10:00 A.M. to 7:00 P.M.; Sunday
11:00 A.M. to 6:00 P.M.

Garden Botanika
Spring Hill Mall
1026 Spring Hill Mall
West Dundee, IL 60118
(847) 426-0790
Hours   Monday through Friday
10:00 A.M. to 9:00 P.M.; Saturday
10:00 A.M. to 6:00 P.M.; Sunday
11:00 A.M. to 6:00 P.M.

General Nutrition Center
Southpoint Plaza
734 E. Rand Road
Arlington Heights, IL 60004
(847) 577-6371
Hours   Monday through Friday
10:00 A.M. to 9:00 P.M.; Saturday
10:00 A.M. to 5:00 P.M.; Sunday
12:00 P.M. to 5:00 P.M.

General Nutrition Center
Woodland Commons
320 W. Half Day Road
Buffalo Grove, IL 60089
(847) 821-9502
Hours   Monday through Thursday 10:00 A.M. to 7:00 P.M.; Friday and Saturday 10:00 A.M. to 6:00 P.M.; Sunday 11:00 A.M. to 4:00 P.M.; First Tuesday of the month 9:00 A.M. to 9:00 P.M.

General Nutrition Center
Crystal Court Plaza
5607 Northwest Highway
Crystal Lake, IL 60014
(815) 356-8336
Hours   Monday through Friday
10:00 A.M. to 8:00 P.M.; Saturday
10:00 A.M. to 6:00 P.M.; Sunday
11:00 A.M. to 5:00 P.M.

General Nutrition Center
Otter Creek Shopping Center
248 S. Randall Road
Elgin, IL 60123
(847) 742-1970
Hours   Monday through Friday
10:00 A.M. to 8:00 P.M.; Saturday
10:00 A.M. to 6:00 P.M.; Sunday
11:00 A.M. to 5:00 P.M.

General Nutrition Center
Evanston Athletic Club
1721 Benson Avenue
Evanston, IL 60201
(847) 864-1698
Hours   Monday through Friday
9:00 A.M. to 9:00 P.M.; Saturday
9:00 A.M. to 6:00 P.M.; Sunday
11:00 A.M. to 5:00 P.M.

General Nutrition Center
Plaza Del Prado
2769 Pfingsten Road
Glenview, IL 60025
(847) 562-0228
Hours   Monday through Friday
10:00 A.M. to 8:00 P.M.; Saturday
10:00 A.M. to 6:00 P.M.; Sunday
11:00 A.M. to 5:00 P.M.

General Nutrition Center
Gurnee Mills
6170 W. Grand Avenue
 Space 163
Gurnee, IL 60031
(847) 855-8654
Hours   Monday through Saturday 10:00 A.M. to 9:00 P.M.; Sunday 11:00 A.M. to 6:00 P.M.

General Nutrition Center
Diet House
1826 Second Street
Highland Park, IL 60035
(847) 433-4766
Hours   Monday through Friday 10:00 A.M. to 6:00 P.M.; Saturday 10:00 A.M. to 5:00 P.M.; Sunday 12:00 P.M. to 5:00 P.M.

General Nutrition Center
Huntley Factory Outlet Shops
11800 Factory Shops Boulevard
Huntley, IL 60142
(847) 669-9129
Hours   Monday through Saturday 10:00 A.M. to 9:00 P.M.; Sunday 10:00 A.M. to 6:00 P.M.

General Nutrition Center
Northlake Commons
307 S. Rand Road
Lake Zurich, IL 60047
(847) 438-2330
Hours   Monday through Friday 10:00 A.M. to 7:00 P.M.; Saturday 10:00 A.M. to 5:00 P.M.; Sunday 12:00 P.M. to 5:00 P.M.

General Nutrition Center
McHenry Plaza
1774 N. Richmond Road
McHenry, IL 60050
(815) 363-8240
Hours   Monday through Friday 10:00 A.M. to 8:00 P.M.; Saturday 10:00 A.M. to 6:00 P.M.; Sunday 11:00 A.M. to 5:00 P.M.

General Nutrition Center
Prairie View Plaza
6725 W. Dempster Street
Morton Grove, IL 60053
(847) 581-1104
Hours   Monday through Friday 10:00 A.M. to 9:00 P.M.; Saturday 10:00 A.M. to 6:00 P.M.; Sunday 11:00 A.M. to 5:00 P.M.

General Nutrition Center
Randhurst Shopping Center
999 N. Elmhurst Road
Mount Prospect, IL 60056
(847) 259-4662
Hours   Monday through Friday 10:00 A.M. to 9:00 P.M.; Saturday 10:00 A.M. to 7:00 P.M.; Sunday 11:00 A.M. to 6:00 P.M.

General Nutrition Center
Golf Mill Shopping Center
249 Golf Mill Center

Niles, IL 60648
(847) 298-3106
Hours   Monday through Saturday 10:00 A.M. to 9:00 P.M.; Sunday 11:00 A.M. to 6:00 P.M.

General Nutrition Center
Northbrook Court
2064 Northbrook Court
Northbrook, IL 60062
(847) 714-9691
Hours   Monday through Friday 10:00 A.M. to 9:00 P.M.; Saturday 10:00 A.M. to 7:00 P.M.; Sunday 11:00 A.M. to 6:00 P.M.

General Nutrition Center
Mallard Creek
740 E. Rollins Road
Round Lake Beach, IL 60073
(847) 740-4337
Hours   Monday through Friday 10:00 A.M. to 7:00 P.M.; Saturday 11:00 A.M. to 5:00 P.M.; Sunday 12:00 P.M. to 5:00 P.M.

General Nutrition Center
Scharrington Square
2447 W. Schaumburg Road
Schaumburg, IL 60194
(847) 891-1350
Hours   Monday through Friday 10:00 A.M. to 9:00 P.M.; Saturday 10:00 A.M. to 5:00 P.M.; Sunday 11:00 A.M. to 5:00 P.M.

General Nutrition Center
Woodfield Mall
Space G-127
Schaumburg, IL 60173
(847) 330-9057
Hours   Monday through Friday 10:00 A.M. to 9:00 P.M.; Saturday 10:00 A.M. to 7:00 P.M.; Sunday 11:00 A.M. to 6:00 P.M.

General Nutrition Center
Village Crossing
5465 W. Touhy Avenue
Skokie, IL 60077
(847) 933-1654
Hours   Monday through Friday 10:00 A.M. to 9:00 P.M.; Saturday 10:00 A.M. to 7:00 P.M.; Sunday 11:00 A.M. to 6:00 P.M.

General Nutrition Center
Hawthorne Center
Vernon Hills, IL 60061
(847) 816-6818
Hours   Monday through Friday 10:00 A.M. to 9:00 P.M.; Saturday 10:00 A.M. to 7:00 P.M.; Sunday 11:00 A.M. to 6:00 P.M.

General Nutrition Center
569 Liberty Square
Wauconda, IL 60084
(847) 487-7904
Hours   Monday through Friday 10:00 A.M. to 8:00 P.M.; Saturday

10:00 A.M. to 6:00 P.M.; Sunday 12:00 P.M. to 5:00 P.M.

General Nutrition Center
Lakehurst Mall
189 Lakehurst Road
Waukegan, IL 60085
(847) 689-3300
Hours   Monday through Friday 10:00 A.M. to 9:00 P.M.; Saturday, Sunday 10:00 A.M. to 6:00 P.M.

General Nutrition Center
Spring Hill Mall
1474 Spring Hill Mall
West Dundee, IL 60118
(847) 426-9253
Hours   Monday through Friday 10:00 A.M. to 9:00 P.M.; Saturday 10:00 A.M. to 6:00 P.M.; Sunday 11:00 A.M. to 6:00 P.M.

General Nutrition Center
Edens Plaza
3232 Lake Avenue, Suite 175
Wilmette, IL 60091
(847) 256-7520
Hours   Monday through Friday 10:00 A.M. to 9:00 P.M.; Saturday 10:00 A.M. to 6:00 P.M.; Sunday 11:00 A.M. to 6:00 P.M.

Mario Tricoci
999 W. Dundee Road
Arlington Heights, IL 60004
(847) 398-2070
Hours   Monday   (Reception desk only) 9:00 A.M. to 5:00 P.M.; Tuesday through Friday 8:00 A.M. to 9:00 P.M.; Saturday and Sunday 8:00 A.M. to 5:00 P.M.

Mario Tricoci
5501 N. Route 31
Crystal Lake, IL 60014
(815) 477-7887
Hours   Monday 9:00 A.M. to 6:00 P.M.; Tuesday through Thursday 9:00 A.M. to 9:00 P.M.; Friday and Saturday 9:00 A.M. to 6:00 P.M.; Sunday 10:00 A.M. to 5:00 P.M.

Mario Tricoci
675 Mall Drive
Schaumburg, IL 60173
(847) 619-7400
Hours   Monday through Friday 9:00 A.M. to 9:00 P.M.; Saturday 8:00 A.M. to 6:00 P.M.; Sunday 10:00 A.M. to 4:00 P.M.

Mario Tricoci
Old Orchard Shopping Center
20 E. Old Orchard Center
Skokie, IL 60077
(847) 568-1000
Hours   Monday through Friday 8:00 A.M. to 9:00 P.M.; Saturday & Sunday 8:00 A.M. to 6:00 P.M.

South/Southwest Suburbs

Bath & Body Works
River Oaks
125 River Oaks Center
Calumet City, IL 60409
(708) 891-0028
Hours   Monday through Friday 10:00 A.M. to 9:00 P.M.; Saturday 10:00 A.M. to 7:00 P.M.; Sunday 11:00 A.M. to 6:00 P.M.

Bath & Body Works
Louis Joliet Mall
3340 Mall Loop Drive
Joliet, IL 60431
(815) 254-7902
Hours   Monday through Friday 10:00 A.M. to 9:00 P.M.; Saturday 10:00 A.M. to 7:00 P.M.; Sunday 11:00 A.M. to 6:00 P.M.

Bath & Body Works
Lincoln Mall
208 Lincoln Mall
Matteson, IL 60443
(708) 748-7701
Hours   Monday through Saturday 10:00 A.M. to 9:00 P.M.; Sunday 11:00 A.M. to 6:00 P.M.

Bath & Body Works
Orland Square Mall
638 Orland Square
Orland Park, IL 60462
(708) 403-4272
Hours   Monday through Friday 10:00 A.M. to 9:00 P.M.; Saturday 10:00 A.M. to 7:00 P.M.; Sunday 11:00 A.M. to 6:00 P.M.

The Body Shop
River Oaks Center
24 River Oaks Center
Calumet City, IL 60409
(708) 862-3515
Hours   Monday through Friday 10:00 A.M. to 9:00 P.M.; Saturday 10:00 A.M. to 7:00 P.M.; Sunday 12:00 P.M. to 6:00 P.M.

The Body Shop
Orland Square Mall
548 Orland Square
Orland Park, IL 60462
(708) 460-0499
Hours   Monday through Friday 10:00 A.M. to 9:00 P.M.; Saturday 10:00 A.M. to 7:00 P.M.; Sunday 11:00 A.M. to 6:00 P.M.

Garden Botanika
Louis Joliet Mall
3340 Mall Loop Drive
Joliet, IL 60431
(815) 436-0691
Hours   Monday through Friday 10:00 A.M. to 9:00 P.M.; Saturday 10:00 A.M. to 7:00 P.M.; Sunday 11:00 A.M. to 6:00 P.M.

Garden Botanika
Orland Square Mall
316 Orland Square
Orland Park, IL 60462
(708) 226-0300
Hours   Monday through Friday
10:00 A.M. to 9:00 P.M.; Saturday
10:00 A.M. to 7:00 P.M.; Sunday
11:00 A.M. to 6:00 P.M.

General Nutrition Center
River Oaks Shopping Center
211 River Oaks Center
Calumet City, IL 60409
(708) 862-4227
Hours   Monday through Friday
10:00 A.M. to 9:00 P.M.; Saturday
10:00 A.M. to 7:00 P.M.; Sunday
10:00 A.M. to 6:00 P.M.

General Nutrition Center
Chicago Ridge Mall
95th Street & Ridge
Chicago Ridge, IL 60415
(708) 499-4310
Hours   Monday through Friday
10:00 A.M. to 9:00 P.M.; Saturday
10:00 A.M. to 7:00 P.M.; Sunday
10:00 A.M. to 6:00 P.M.

General Nutrition Center
River Crest Shopping Center
4843 W. Cal-Sag Road
Crestwood, IL 60445
(708) 489-2313
Hours   Monday through Friday
10:00 A.M. to 8:00 P.M.; Saturday
10:00 A.M. to 6:00 P.M.; Sunday
12:00 P.M. to 5:00 P.M.

General Nutrition Center
Evergreen Plaza
9531 Western Avenue
Evergreen Park, IL 60642
(708) 499-4306
Hours   Monday through Friday
10:00 A.M. to 9:00 P.M.; Saturday
10:00 A.M. to 7:00 P.M.; Sunday
11:00 A.M. to 6:00 P.M.

General Nutrition Center
Louis Joliet Mall
3340 Mall Loop Drive
Joliet, IL 60435
(815) 439-1160
Hours   Monday through Friday
10:00 A.M. to 9:00 P.M.; Saturday
10:00 A.M. to 7:00 P.M.; Sunday
11:00 A.M. to 6:00 P.M.

General Nutrition Center
The Wilderness Mall
2450 W. Jefferson Street
Joliet, IL 60435
(815) 744-4191
Hours   Monday through Friday
10:00 A.M. to 9:00 P.M.; Saturday
9:30 A.M. to 5:30 P.M.; Sunday
11:00 A.M. to 5:00 P.M.

General Nutrition Center
Lincoln Mall
108 Lincoln Mall
Matteson, IL 60443
(708) 481-2066
Hours   Monday through Friday
10:00 A.M. to 9:00 P.M.; Saturday
10:00 A.M. to 9:00 P.M.; Sunday
11:00 A.M. to 6:00 P.M.

General Nutrition Center
Orland Square Mall
564 Orland Square
Orland Park, IL 60462
(708) 403-4227
Hours   Monday through Friday
10:00 A.M. to 9:00 P.M.; Saturday
10:00 A.M. to 7:00 P.M.; Sunday
11:00 A.M. to 6:00 P.M.

General Nutrition Center
Tinley Park Plaza
15927 S. Harlem Avenue
Tinley Park, IL 60477
(708) 633-0733
Hours   Monday through Friday
9:30 A.M. to 9:00 P.M.; Saturday
9:00 A.M. to 6:00 P.M.; Sunday
11:00 A.M. to 5:00 P.M.

Mario Tricoci
15451 S. 94th Avenue
Orland Park, IL 60462
(708) 403-4434

Hours   Monday through Friday
8:00 A.M. to 9:00 P.M.; Saturday
8:00 A.M. to 6:00 P.M.; Sunday
10:00 A.M. to 5:00 P.M.

Western Suburbs

Bath & Body Works
Fox Valley Center
1390 Fox Valley Center Drive
Aurora, IL 60504
(630) 978-4742
Hours   Monday through Friday
10:00 A.M. to 9:00 P.M.; Saturday
11:00 A.M. to 6:00 P.M.; Sunday
11:00 A.M. to 6:00 P.M.

Bath & Body Works
Stratford Square
730 Stratford Square
Bloomingdale, IL 60108
(630) 671-1024
Hours   Monday through Friday
10:00 A.M. to 9:00 P.M.; Saturday
10:00 A.M. to 7:00 P.M.; Sunday
11:00 A.M. to 5:00 P.M.

Bath & Body Works
Yorktown Center
203 Yorktown Center
Lombard, IL 60148
(630) 424-1270
Hours   Monday through Friday
10:00 A.M. to 9:00 P.M.; Saturday

10:00 A.M. to 7:00 P.M.; Sunday 11:00 A.M. to 6:00 P.M.

Bath & Body Works
Harlem Irving Plaza
4190 N. Harlem Avenue
Norridge, IL 60634
(708) 452-3698
Hours   Monday through Saturday 10:00 A.M. to 9:00 P.M.; Sunday 11:00 A.M. to 6:00 P.M.

Bath & Body Works
North Riverside Park Mall
7501 W. Cermak Road
North Riverside, IL 60546
(708) 442-3473
Hours   Monday through Friday 10:00 A.M. to 9:00 P.M.; Saturday 10:00 A.M. to 7:00 P.M.; Sunday 11:00 A.M. to 6:00 P.M.

Bath & Body Works
Oak Brook Center
35 Oak Brook Center
Oak Brook, IL 60523
(630) 954-2878
Hours   Monday through Friday 10:00 A.M. to 9:00 P.M.; Saturday 10:00 A.M. to 7:00 P.M.; Sunday 11:00 A.M. to 6:00 P.M.

Bath & Body Works
Charlestown Mall
3802 E. Main Street
St. Charles, IL 60174
(630) 443-7292
Hours   Monday through Saturday 10:00 A.M. to 9:00 P.M.; Sunday 11:00 A.M. to 6:00 P.M.

Bath & Body Works
Wheaton Town Square
111 Town Square
Wheaton, IL 60187
(630) 653-6019
Hours   Monday through Friday 10:00 A.M. to 9:00 P.M.; Saturday 10:00 A.M. to 6:00 P.M.; Sunday 11:00 A.M. to 5:00 P.M.

Bath & Body Works
Woodridge Festival
1001 W. 75th Street
Woodridge, IL 60517
(630) 910-7015
Hours   Monday through Friday 10:00 A.M. to 9:00 P.M.; Saturday 10:00 A.M. to 6:00 P.M.; Sunday 11:00 A.M. to 5:00 P.M.

The Body Shop
Fox Valley Center
1408 Fox Valley Center Drive
Aurora, IL 60504
(630) 820-8800
Hours   Monday through Friday 10:00 A.M. to 9:00 P.M.; Saturday

10:00 A.M. to 7:00 P.M.; Sunday
11:00 A.M. to 6:00 P.M.

The Body Shop
Stratford Square
206 Stratford Square
Bloomingdale, IL 60108
(630) 893-3551
Hours   Monday through Friday
10:00 A.M. to 9:00 P.M.; Saturday
10:00 A.M. to 7:00 P.M.; Sunday
11:00 A.M. to 6:00 P.M.

Crabtree & Evelyn
Oak Brook Center
420 Oak Brook Center
Oak Brook, IL 60523
(630) 571-8445
Hours   Monday through Friday
10:00 A.M. to 9:00 P.M.; Saturday
10:00 A.M. to 7:00 P.M.; Sunday
11:00 A.M. to 6:00 P.M.

Garden Botanika
Fox Valley Center
2162 Fox Valley Center Drive
Aurora, IL 60504
(630) 898-2072
Hours   Monday through Friday
10:00 A.M. to 9:00 P.M.; Saturday
10:00 A.M. to 6:00 P.M.; Sunday
11:00 A.M. to 6:00 P.M.

Garden Botanika
Yorktown Center
229 Yorktown Center
Lombard, IL 60148
(630) 620-9128
Hours   Monday through Friday
10:00 A.M. to 9:00 P.M.; Saturday
10:00 A.M. to 7:00 P.M.; Sunday
11:00 A.M. to 6:00 P.M.

General Nutrition Center
Fox Valley Center
2356 Fox Valley Center Drive
Aurora, IL 60504
(630) 898-5284
Hours   Monday through Friday
10:00 A.M. to 9:00 P.M.; Saturday
10:00 A.M. to 6:00 P.M.; Sunday
11:00 A.M. to 6:00 P.M.

General Nutrition Center
Shoppes at Windmill Place
53 S. Randall Road
Batavia, IL 60510
(630) 879-8252
Hours   Monday through Friday
10:00 A.M. to 8:00 P.M.; Saturday
10:00 A.M. to 5:00 P.M.; Sunday
12:00 P.M. to 5:00 P.M.

General Nutrition Center
Springbrook Shopping Center
156-J E. Lake Street
Bloomingdale, IL 60108
(630) 582-0959
Hours   Monday through Friday
10:00 A.M. to 9:00 P.M.; Saturday
10:00 A.M. to 5:00 P.M.; Sunday
11:00 A.M. to 5:00 P.M.

General Nutrition Center
Stratford Square
816 Stratford Square
Bloomingdale, IL 60108
(630) 307-9156
Hours   Monday through Friday 10:00 A.M. to 9:00 P.M.; Saturday 10:00 A.M. to 7:00 P.M.; Sunday 11:00 A.M. to 6:00 P.M.

General Nutrition Center
Maple Park Plaza
283 N. Naperville Road
Bolingbrook, IL 60440
(630) 378-9670
Hours   Monday through Friday 10:00 A.M. to 8:00 P.M.; Saturday, Sunday 12:00 P.M. to 5:00 P.M.

General Nutrition Center
Broadview Village Square
128 Broadview Village Square
Broadview, IL 60153
(708) 343-5053
Hours   Monday through Friday 10:00 A.M. to 8:00 P.M.; Saturday 10:00 A.M. to 6:00 P.M.; Sunday 11:00 A.M. to 5:00 P.M.

General Nutrition Center
Downers Grove Park Plaza
7313 Lemont Road
Downers Grove, IL 60516
(630) 515-9410
Hours   Monday through Friday 10:00 A.M. to 9:00 P.M.; Saturday 10:00 A.M. to 6:00 P.M.; Sunday 12:00 P.M. to 5:00 P.M.

General Nutrition Center
Market Plaza
585 Roosevelt Road
Glen Ellyn, IL 60137
(630) 469-3438
Hours   Monday through Friday 10:00 A.M. to 8:00 P.M.; Saturday 10:00 A.M. to 5:00 P.M.; Sunday 12:00 P.M. to 5:00 P.M.

General Nutrition Center
Quarry Mall
9320 Joliet Road
Hodgkins, IL 60525
(708) 485-7290
Hours   Monday through Friday 9:30 A.M. to 9:00 P.M.; Saturday 9:30 A.M. to 6:00 P.M.; Sunday 11:00 A.M. to 5:00 P.M.

General Nutrition Center
Yorktown Center
201 Yorktown Center
Lombard, IL 60148
(630) 916-9022
Hours   Monday through Friday 10:00 A.M. to 9:00 P.M.; Saturday 10:00 A.M. to 7:00 P.M.; Sunday 11:00 A.M. to 6:00 P.M.

General Nutrition Center
Ogden Mall
1255 E. Ogden Avenue

Naperville, IL 60563
(630) 428-1462
Hours   Monday through Friday
10:00 A.M. to 8:30 P.M.; Saturday
10:00 A.M. to 5:00 P.M.; Sunday
12:00 P.M. to 5:00 P.M.

General Nutrition Center
North Riverside Park Mall
7501 W. Cermak
North Riverside, IL 60546
(708) 447-5160
Hours   Monday through Friday
10:00 A.M. to 9:00 P.M.; Saturday
10:00 A.M. to 7:00 P.M.; Sunday
11:00 A.M. to 6:00 P.M.

General Nutrition Center
Oak Brook Center
525 Oak Brook Center
Oak Brook, IL 60523
(630) 586-0064
Hours   Monday through Friday
10:00 A.M. to 9:30 P.M.; Saturday
11:00 A.M. to 7:00 P.M.; Sunday
11:00 A.M. to 6:00 P.M.

General Nutrition Center
Townes Crossing
2458 Route 30
Oswego, IL 60543
(630) 844-2576
Hours   Monday through Friday
10:00 A.M. to 8:30 P.M.; Saturday
10:00 A.M. to 7:30 P.M.; Sunday
12:00 P.M. to 5:00 P.M.

General Nutrition Center
Charlestown Mall
3800 E. Main Street
St. Charles, IL 60174
(630) 377-1885
Hours   Monday through Friday
10:00 A.M. to 9:00 P.M.; Saturday
10:00 A.M. to 9:00 P.M.; Sunday
11:00 A.M. to 6:00 P.M.

General Nutrition Center
North Park Mall
North Street and Route 64
Villa Park, IL 60181
(630) 834-6864
Hours   Monday through Friday
10:00 A.M. to 9:00 P.M.; Saturday
10:00 A.M. to 6:00 P.M.; Sunday
11:00 A.M. to 5:00 P.M.

General Nutrition Center
Westbrook Commons
3030 S. Wolf Road
Westchester, IL 60154
(708) 562-7686
Hours   Monday through Friday
10:00 A.M. to 8:00 P.M.; Saturday
10:00 A.M. to 5:00 P.M.; Sunday
12:00 P.M. to 5:00 P.M.

General Nutrition Center
92 Danada Square West
Wheaton, IL 60187
(630) 260-9323
Hours   Monday through Friday
10:00 A.M. to 8:00 P.M.; Saturday

10:00 A.M. to 5:00 P.M.; Sunday 12:00 P.M. to 5:00 P.M.

General Nutrition Center
Wood Dale Center
357 W. Irving Park Road
Wood Dale, IL 60101
(630) 238-9522
Hours   Monday through Friday 10:00 A.M. to 9:00 P.M.; Saturday 10:00 A.M. to 5:00 P.M.; Sunday 11:00 A.M. to 5:00 P.M.

Mario Tricoci
64 Stratford Drive
Bloomingdale, IL 60108
(630) 980-5900
Hours   Monday through Friday 9:00 A.M. to 9:00 P.M.; Saturday 9:00 A.M. to 6:00 P.M.; Sunday 10:00 A.M. to 5:00 P.M.

Mario Tricoci
1504 Naperville Boulevard
Naperville, IL 60563
(630) 955-0050
Hours   Monday through Friday 8:00 A.M. to 9:00 P.M.; Saturday 8:00 A.M. to 6:00 P.M.; Sunday 10:00 A.M. to 5:00 P.M.

Mario Tricoci
Oak Brook Center
284 Oak Brook Center
Oak Brook, IL 60523
(630) 572-0500
Hours   Monday through Friday 9:00 A.M. to 9:00 P.M.; Saturday 9:00 A.M. to 6:00 P.M.; Sunday 10:00 A.M. to 5:00 P.M.

Glossary

Acupressure A treatment used in Chinese medicine that involves the use of finger pressure rather than needles at specific points along the body to treat conditions such as tension, chronic pain, arthritis, and menstrual cramps.

Acupuncture A technique most commonly used in traditional Chinese medicine in which fine needles are placed in certain areas of the body to stimulate or disperse the flow of chi, or energy, to restore the body to its healthy state. Acupuncture is often used to treat chronic and degenerative conditions.

Advanced Energy Healing A type of spiritual healing discovered by Robert T. Jaffe, M.D., this technique is an energetic approach to healing that empowers people to understand and transform the energy and consciousness that create disease. This healing works at the causative level of disease, teaching both the healer and the patient to understand the relationship between disease, consciousness, and the multiple levels of energy that create health and healing.

Alexander Technique Best regarded as a reeducation process rather than a healing treatment, the Alexander Technique was developed by Australian actor Frederick Matthias Alexander, who observed a relationship between his poor posture and the frequent loss of his voice. Practitioners of this technique instruct patients on more efficient ways of moving their bodies that result in an improvement of posture, balance, and coordination. It also helps eliminate pain and stress.

Applied Kinesiology A type of diagnostic technique that uses muscle testing to gain information about a patient's health.

Aromatherapy This treatment involves the use of essential oils derived from plants to treat emotional disorders such as stress and anxiety. It has also been used to ease chronic conditions such as asthma. These oils can be inhaled or massaged into the skin and are sometimes placed in baths. Aromatherapy is often used with other therapies such as acupuncture, reflexology, chiropractic treatment, and massage.

Ashtanga Vinyasa yoga This style of yoga is more vigorous than classical Hatha yoga. It involves long flowing movements in which each asana, or posture, is connected with a series of sun salutations. Another aspect that distinguishes this style from Hatha yoga is that for each pose there is a counter pose and each asana is held for five breaths.

Ayurvedic Medicine The traditional system of medicine practiced in India and Sri Lanka, this five-thousand-year-old healing art involves the use of herbs, diet, exercise, detoxification, meditation, and other modalities to treat various conditions ranging from allergies to AIDS. One of the cornerstone beliefs of Ayurvedic medicine is that everything in the universe is composed of prana, or energy, and that human beings are also bundles of energy. The practitioner's skill lies in his or her ability to identify a person's constitution or body type, diagnose the causes of imbalance, and then prescribe the appropriate treatment.

Biofeedback A technique used for stress-related conditions that involves monitoring the metabolic changes in the body with the aid of a highly sensitive machine. During this treatment, patients also learn techniques to bring the body back to a more calm state.

Chelation Therapy This treatment involves intravenous injections of the synthetic amino acid EDTA to detoxify the body and to treat certain conditions like arteriosclerosis.

Chinese Medicine Practitioners of this healing art use a variety of ancient and contemporary methods to treat patients including acupuncture, herbs, massage, moxibustion (a kind of heat therapy), and nutritional counseling.

Chiropractic Medicine Practitioners of this system of medicine believe that the misalignment of the spine puts pressure on the spinal nerve roots, causing a variety of health problems. The chiropractor seeks to correct the misalignment through spinal manipulation or adjustment. Two specialized forms of chiropractic include National Upper Cervical (NUCCA) that involves adjustments to the upper neck, and Network Chiropractic that involves more gentle adjustments.

Colon Therapy A method that cleanses the intestinal tract of the buildup of toxins, waste, and bacteria. Colon therapists perform colonic irrigations, or colonics, using water or herbal tinctures.

Craniosacral Therapy This therapy involves the manual manipulation of the bones in the skull to balance the cerebrospinal fluid—a clear watery substance surrounding the brain and spinal cord, regarded by one of the therapy's founders as "the highest known element in the human body." This extremely gentle treatment is often recommended for children suffering with colic, fretfulness, spinal curvatures, and breathing problems. It's also an excellent treatment for hyperactivity.

Craniosacral therapy has helped adults who suffer with sinus problems, head, neck, and spine injuries, and migraines.

Deep-Tissue Body Work A range of manipulation therapies designed to improve the function of the body's connective tissues or muscles.

Energy Field Work A range of therapies that may or may not involve the laying-on of hands, this treatment can have an effect on the patient's physical, mental, and spiritual well-being. After identifying weaknesses in and around the patient's energy field, the practitioner works to restore the body back to balance by channeling energy to strengthen the patient's natural defenses.

Environmental Medicine This is a system of medicine in which the practitioner checks for the existence of allergens or chemical toxins in the patient's diet or in his or her immediate environment. The goal of this treatment is to free the body of these elements so that the body can heal.

Feldenkrais Method This treatment combines movement training, gentle touch, and verbal instruction to help clients create a more free, efficient way of moving their body. There are two parts involved in this treatment: individual sessions wherein the practitioner's touch is used to address the student's breathing and body alignment and a series of classes wherein clients engage in slow, nonaerobic motions called awareness through movement. This method is frequently used to treat stress and tension and to prevent recurring injury.

Feng Shui The Chinese practice of configuring the home or workplace to promote health, prosperity, and happiness.

Flower Essences Made popular in the 1930s by Edward Bach, M.D., this treatment focuses on the client's emotional state rather than the illness. Flower essences are taken orally and can be placed underneath the tongue or mixed in a beverage. The essences help alleviate negative emotional states that can contribute to illness or stunt personal growth.

Hakomi This is a kind of mind/body-oriented psychotherapy that integrates mindfulness in getting to the root of emotional problems. During this therapy, the practitioner watches the way the patient's body reacts to certain stimuli and encourages the patient to work with rather than against the body's natural movement.

Hawaiian Energetics A traditional Hawaiian healing art that utilizes the elemental energies of fire, air, earth, and water, this therapy includes physical techniques, energetic healing, and spiritual practices in addressing life situations.

Herbalism This treatment uses natural plants or plant-based substances to treat illnesses. It's also used to enhance the body's functioning. Several holistic practitioners such as acupuncturists and naturopaths as well as holistic chiropractors, physicians, and dentists use herbs to treat their clients.

Homeopathy A system of medicine in which small doses of remedies, or natural substances, are used to stimulate a person's immune system. These remedies, if given in larger doses, could cause the same physical or psychological symptoms from which the patient is suffering. Practitioners who specialize in this healing method are called homeopaths.

Hypnotherapy This refers to a variety of techniques used to help the client access the subconscious mind where suppressed memories, emotions, and experiences have been recorded.

Kemetic yoga A style of yoga that is believed to have been practiced in ancient Egypt, this system of exercise emphasizes the correlation between breathing and movement. In Kemetic yoga, one posture, or movement, is connected to another in a geometric progression. The postures are based upon forms and positions that are represented on Egyptian hieroglyphics, wall paintings, and carvings.

Lomi Lomi Traditional Hawaiian massage taught by Auntie Margaret Machado from the big island of Hawaii where the practitioner uses rhythmic strokes and stretching to remove energy blocks and tension from the body.

Massage This is a touch therapy involving the manipulation of the body's soft tissue in which the practitioner uses his or her hands to detect tightness in the muscles, ligaments, and tendons. One of the most popular forms of massage in this country is the Swedish massage, a treatment that involves long flowing strokes on various areas of the body. Massage therapy also incorporates other therapeutic techniques such as reflexology, aromatherapy, and trigger point therapy, the concentrated use of finger pressure on painful, irritated areas in the muscles.

Meditation This technique consists of a variety of practices that encourage the participant to develop inner silence and reflection. Some methods involve focused breathing while other methods involve visualization. However, there are some techniques that require the participant to just sit in silence. Meditation is often undertaken by people who want to reduce stress or are in search of spiritual clarity.

Myofascial Release This hands-on technique involves working with the fascia, or connective tissue, and is sometimes used by body workers to treat recurring sports injuries, neck and back pain, and headaches.

Naprapathy A form of therapy founded in Chicago by Dr. Oakley Smith in 1905, this treatment involves gentle therapeutic manipulations of the ligaments and muscles, supporting structures of the spine, and connective tissue. Professionals in this field, who are called naprapaths, believe that the body has natural healing capabilities and that manipulation therapy assists the self-healing process.

Naturopathic Medicine A system of medicine that relies upon natural healing modalities such as herbal medicine, homeopathic remedies, lifestyle changes, and nutritional counseling to restore the body to good health. Professionals in this field are called naturopaths.

Neuro-Linguistic Programming Commonly referred to as NLP, this technique helps alter limiting thought, language, and behavior patterns. During sessions, practitioners watch the client's posture, language, eye movement, and breathing pattern and then assist him or her in changing these habits for an improved emotional state.

Osteopathic Medicine Like medical doctors, these healthcare professionals prescribe medication, perform surgery, and make hospital referrals. The difference between them and medical doctors is that doctors of osteopathic medicine look at the patient's joints, bones, nerves, and muscles for clues regarding the patient's overall health. They are also trained in osteopathic manipulation, a hand technique used to diagnose and treat illness and disease.

Phoenix Rising Yoga Therapy This therapy involves a combination of yoga techniques and modern psychology. During a session, practitioners assist clients with guided breathing and yoga postures which are believed to help release subconscious emotions or beliefs that appear in the body as chronic aches or pains.

Qi Gong Also known as chi-kung, this Chinese system of exercise stimulates and balances the flow of qi, or energy, along acupuncture meridians. It is often used to improve blood circulation, alleviate stress, and improve immunity. This exercise system is often taught in conjunction with tai chi.

Raja yoga Also known as "quieting the mind," Raja yoga refers to the meditative aspect of yoga. In addition to a regular practice of sitting in silence, students are also encouraged to become more conscious, or meditative, in their everyday lives.

Reflexology Also known as zone therapy, this technique is based upon the belief that points on the feet and hand correspond to tissues and organs throughout the body. During a treatment session, the practitioner applies pressure to different areas on the feet or hands with their fingers and thumbs. This helps rid the body of pain and tension.

Reiki An ancient healing art in which the practitioner channels energy to the client using light hand placements around weakened areas of the body, Reiki can be used for emotional and physical discomfort as well as for spiritual clarity.

Rolfing Developed in the 1930s by biochemist Ida Rolf, this technique is based upon the philosophy that a body that functions with the force of gravity is capable of healing itself. Treatment involves ten sixty- to ninety-minute sessions wherein the practitioner manipulates the connective tissue or fascia. Rolfing does not cure any particular disease per se, but it can help promote emotional release, relieve chronic back, neck, and shoulder pain, plus alleviate asthma and digestive problems.

Shiatsu This is a Japanese treatment that is similar to acupuncture except practitioners use their fingers, palms, knees, feet, arms, and elbows instead of needles to apply pressure to points in the body called tsubo. The goal of the practitioner is to unblock these energy centers and stimulate ki, the Japanese word for energy. Shiatsu is used to relieve stress, stimulate the circulatory and immune system, and relax the nervous system. It is also good for back pain, headaches, and digestive problems.

Spiritual Healing A kind of therapy that involves a practitioner, or healer, who acts as a channel through which healing energy from the one universal divine source is directed to the recipient. This healing energy has an intelligence of its own and automatically goes where it is needed. It can affect an individual on the emotional, physical, and spiritual level. Although there are several different types of spiritual healing, Barbara Brennan's method of healing is a formalized program of this healing art. Shamanic healing also fits in this category.

Structural Integration A ten-session manipulation therapy in which the practitioner uses his or her hands, arms, and elbows on the fascia, or connective tissue, while the client is directed in deep breathing techniques. The goal of this treatment is to correct misalignment in the body created by gravity, physical problems, and emotional distress.

Tai Chi Chuan An ancient, noncombative martial art that involves slow, graceful movements performed in a definite pattern combined with breath work. Tai chi is a part of the traditional Chinese medicine system and is used to promote longevity and spiritual awareness.

Therapeutic Touch This is a holistic therapy designed by and used by nurses in which the practitioner uses his or her hands to channel energy to a weak or congested area on the patient's body to bring it back into balance.

Watsu A healing type of massage performed in water by a practitioner who guides the client through a variety of movements while using stretches and finger pressure that help dissolve energy blockages in the body. This treatment is used to relieve tension and also alleviates a variety of emotional and physical problems. This is also known as water Shiatsu.

Yoga An exercise system that benefits the mind, body, and spirit, some forms of yoga emphasize perfect posture and alignment of the body while others encourage a connection to a higher consciousness. Hatha yoga, one of the most popular forms of yoga in the United States, emphasizes the importance of good posture, breathing, and meditation. One form of Hatha yoga, Iyengar, incorporates the use of props. Ashtanga Vinyasa yoga is yet another traditional form.

Zero Balancing Often used for reducing stress, this treatment seeks to align body structure and body energy. Similar to acupressure, it involves the use of touch to help overcome imbalances in the body's structure and energy field.